PITS

A PICTORIAL RECORD OF MINING

PITS

A PICTORIAL RECORD OF MINING

John Threlkeld

Wharncliffe Publishing Limited

Front cover: Seventy-five miners were killed in an explosion at Darley Main Colliery, Worsbrough Dale, on 24 January, 1849. Many of the bodies were 'shockingly disfigured', according to a report carried in the *Illustrated London News*. The inquest was told that not only had the ventilation been bad, but large holes had been left in which foul air and gas accumulated, and in places there were no currents of air. Some of the miners had been using candles.

First published in 1994 by
Wharncliffe Publishing Limited
47 Church Street, Barnsley
South Yorkshire S70 2AS

© John Threlkeld, 1994

For up-to-date information about other titles produced under the Wharncliffe Publishing imprint, please telephone or write to:

Wharncliffe Publishing Limited
FREEPOST
47 Church Street, Barnsley
South Yorkshire S70 2AS
Telephone (24 hours): (01226) 734555

ISBN   1 871647 23 1

Printed by Yorkshire Web, Barnsley, South Yorkshire.

Contents

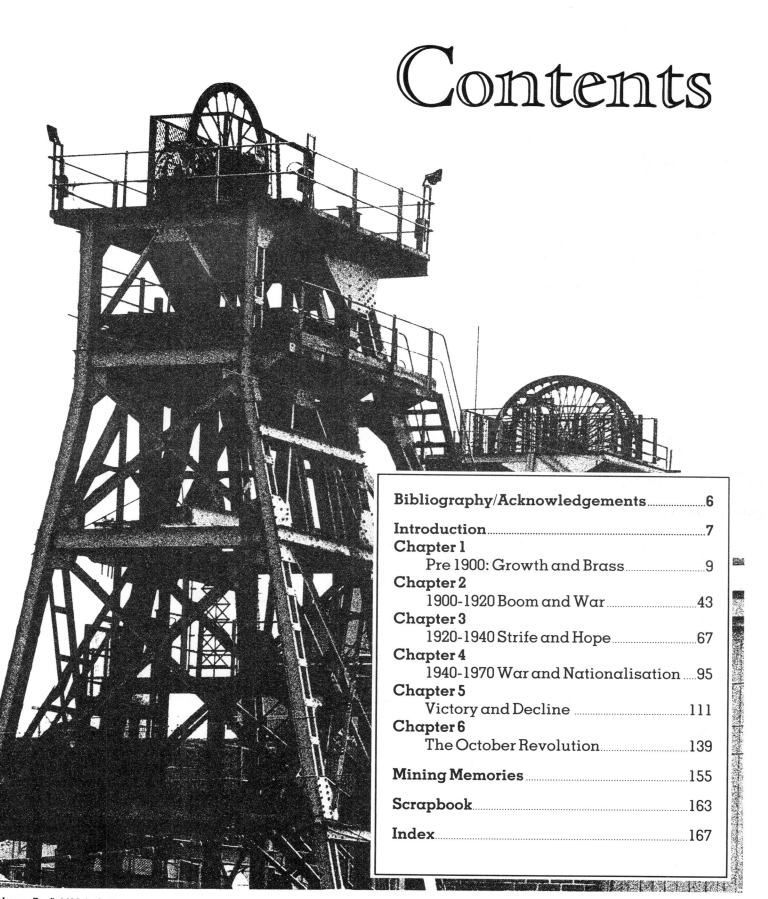

Above: Darfield Main Colliery

Acknowledgements

My thanks to Helen Williams, the family of Frank Ashton, Ian Harley, Carolyn Thorpe, June Walton, Paul Greenan, Josie Clark, Jim Marsden, George Beedan, Rosemary Preece, Mrs. P. Greaves, Mr. and Mrs. R. Firth, John Goodchild, Mr. F. Williamson, Mr. J. Gill, Mrs. R. Hirst, Roni Wilkinson, Wes Hobson, Jenny Wood, Don Oakes, Alan Billingham, Lord Mason, Mr. J. McKenning, Doncaster Borough Council, Barnsley Library (Local Studies), Ruth Vyse, Sheffield Library (Archives) Department, British Coal Public Relations Department and the Yorkshire NUM (Phil Thompson and Tom Bellamy).

Bibliography

Ten Year Stint, A. Robens
The Miners (series), R.P. Arnot
Historical Directory of Trade Unions, Arthur Marsh and Victoria Ryan
The Yorkshire Miners, Frank Machin
Coals from Barnsley, John Goodchild
The Changing Role of the Miners Rescue Team, G.V. Jollife
Report of Mining in Silkstone, 1901, G. H. Teasdale
Report on the explosion at Wharncliffe Woodmoor 1/2/3., Government Mines Department
Report on the explosion at Barnsley main, Ministry of Fuel and Power
Scargill and the Miners, Michael Crick
The Coal Scuttle, Joseph Jones
Scargill: The Unauthorized Biography, Paul Routledge
Barnsley Record and Barnsley Chronicle files.

Right: Barnsley Main

Introduction

The first Pits book was published in 1987 and there have been no reprints since the publication of Pits 2 in 1989, although there has been a constant demand for the first book. 1993 was considered to be an appropriate time to re-launch the book, since this year has seen the closure of the last pits in what had been the Barnsley coalfield, Grimethorpe and Houghton Main. As well as producing a new chapter, on the "People's Revolt" against the October, 1992, pit closure programme, we decided to enlarge the early chapters; the new material includes photographs from the Yorkshire Mining Museum. The result is a revised and enlarged book which offers almost all of the original material — unfortunately some of the photographs have faded and therefore cannot be used again — and new chapters aimed at presenting the nineteenth century miner (see *The Early Miner*) and the pre-second world war miner (see *Men of Iron*) from another viewpoint. What made them tick? Why were they seen to be different from the rest of society?

Unfortunately, some of the chapters overlap and this has been unavoidable, *Men of Iron*, for instance, has been included in the pre-1920 chapter but some of the paragraphs refer to later decades. It was decided to put them together to maintain continuity of theme, i.e the miners' relationship with the physical side of the job and with his environment below and above ground, rather than spread the paragraphs across a number of chapters.

The chapter on the miners' strike of 1984/85 has been beefed up. Next March sees the tenth anniversary of the start of the strike which broke the power of the NUM and set the stage for the dismantling of the coal industry. With the help of hindsight I have re-structured that chapter to pinpoint post-strike trends which were not discernible in 1987.

Above all the book is a tribute to coal miners. In many respects they were extraordinary men whose lives were based on muscle power and stoicism. In the past ten years there has been a revolution on the work front and jobs have vanished in what were considered to be secure and 'men only' domains, in steel, the docks, the armed forces, the building trade as well as coal mining. In physical terms this is the era of the soft job (if you are fortunate enough to have one), in the office, warehouse, factory and shop, with the result that these characters who earned their living working in dirty and primitive conditions underground, relying on muscles and their wits, will soon seem to belong to another species.

Chapter 1

Pre 1900: Growth and Brass

Mining is seen as a relatively modern industry with its roots in the industrial revolution but in Silkstone mining was an old industry 200 years before the Norman Conquest. When the Abbot of Peterborough gave a grant of land for the digging of coal in 833 he probably thought he was one of a new breed of entrepreneurs who would blaze a new trail by exploiting this early version of a privatised coal mine; however, when the workers arrived on the scene they found the local inhabitants had been mining for years and there were outcrops all over the countryside: an example of local enterprise, 833-style!

In 1370 several leases for coal working at Corkworth, near Wentworth, were awarded to the Fitzwilliam family at Wentworth Woodhouse, who later became one of the major pit owners in Barnsley, running mines at Elsecar, Jump and Hemingfield. The Court Rolls of Wakefield contain an entry in 1308 that a licence was granted to dig for coal at Hipperholme, near Wakefield, and by the beginning of the fifteenth century, coal mining was an established industry in Wakefield. Yorkshire coal was used for the burning of lime needed to build York Minster, and the Fabric Rolls show a payment in 1499 for the purchase of coal from Wakefield. At about the same time the Cluniac Monks of Pontefract acquired a coal pit at Barnsley for eight pounds, the estimated life of which was sixteen years and there was primitive mining in Gawber in the 1500s. But the industry did not expand until the middle of the seventeenth century, when coal came into general use. A local newspaper, speculating on the sluggish expansion of the industry in the sixteenth century, stated in the 1870s: "This was no doubt attributable to the plentiful supply of wood. Not that the inhabitants were so long ignorant of this mineral, but wood was easily procured, and our ancestors not having the advantages of the mechanised contrivances by which coal is now so readily won, we can at once excuse them from putting forth great efforts for its acquisition."

That was not the full story. Mining has always aroused controversy and until the mid-seventeenth century there were objections on the grounds of air pollution and public safety. In 1306, 650 years before the infamous London smogs of the 1950s and nearly 700 years before pollution and the greenhouse effect became fashionable, Parliament petitioned the King to try to prohibit the use of the fuel, as it polluted the air, and the authorities clamped down on mining operations. One man was tried, convicted and hanged for burning coal. There was opposition in Barnsley as well. In 1413, five men were fined for extracting coal without permission at Darton. Two hundred years later, again at Darton, Michael Wentworth was fined because he had not covered up old coal pits on the common. Opposition subsided but even in 1659 no coal could be mined at Clayton West at haytime.

The first known pit explosion in Barnsley occurred in 1672, resulting in the death of James Townend, who lived in Silkstone. In 1693 Abraham Rock leased part of Keresforth Farm for coal getting, at an annual rent of seventeen pounds; four years later there were coal pits at Gawber Hall. In 1714, according to Thoresby's History of Leeds, the pits were "now without number." South Yorkshire was described as "black with coal pits and the smoke of fire engines, but with good land, and with many gentlemen's seats." Bell-pits, so called because on reaching coal the workings were widened in the form of a bell, were in use in 1728. Other developments: in 1776 John Curr, of Sheffield, who was the manager of the Duke of Norfolk's collieries, substituted trams running on cast-iron rails for the sledges then in use for transporting coals; the first shaft of any great depth in Barnsley was sunk by James Clarke about 1790, near Noblethorpe, the coal being brought out in baskets. Coal was consumed locally and went by land on the back of a pack horse or cart. It was still a small industry, heading in the right direction but without an efficient transport system to move the coal around the country. The industry expanded when the nation embarked on the industrial revolution.

There were three growth villages in Barnsley: Silkstone, Elsecar and Gawber, all dominated by families who worked alone: the Clarkes (Silkstone), the Fitzwilliams (Elsecar) and the Thorps (Gawber). Such was the significance of Silkstone in the early development of mining in this area that a seam

stretching from the outskirts of Leeds to Alfreton in Derbyshire derived its name from the village. In 1804 Mr Clarke was corresponding with captains of ships and London merchants with a view to sending coal to the capital. A cargo was delivered to London on July 29, 1805, via canals to Goole, where it was transhipped into a sloop but the costs were too high to establish trade at that time. Nothing could stop the formidable Clarkes when the railways arrived. In 1846 the Manchester and Sheffield line was opened for coal traffic, and Mrs Clarke sent the first train of coal through the Woodhead Tunnel from Oxspring to Tintwistle. The 1851 Exhibition in Hyde Park put Silkstone coal firmly on the map, the family having sent a three hundredweight lump of coal to the exhibition for display purposes and it caused a sensation, resulting in the family's coal becoming well-known in London and throughout the country. Three years later the Worsbrough branch of the South Yorkshire Railway Company which went through the

Dove Valley as far as Moorend Colliery, belonging to Mrs Clarke, was opened.

The Thorps were almost as resourceful as the Clarkes: they were selling coal in Barnsley between 1805 and 1809. Samuel Thorp, of Gawber Hall (demolished in the 1930s due to mining subsidence) and Banks Hall, Cawthorne, was the first man to work the Barnsley seam on a large scale, at Cobbler Hole Pit, and the family had at various stages pits at Stainborough, Honeywell and Willowbank. Gawber is still riddled with old mine workings. The third family, the Fitzwilliams, members of the landed gentry who boasted of close links with Royalty, monopolised coal mining in Elsecar, having taken advantage of the opening of the Dearne and Dove canal in 1805. At about that time it was said that the Elsecar pit was so clean and spacious that sometimes the ladies from Wentworth Woodhouse, the largest country house in the nation, and owned by the Fitzwilliams, went down the pit to witness the

10

Above: Canal barges at Elsecar pre-1900. Elsecar was one of the growth villages in South Yorkshire. *John Goodchild Collection, Wakefield.*

operations. The Fitzwilliams were humane proprietors who provided decent housing and decent working conditions, although some pit managers grumbled that some of the employees expected jobs for life which, they said, was not conducive to healthy competition and business! With the growth of the railways, the most significant development in the opening up of the local coalfields, some of the leading pit proprietors formed a trading company under the title Silkstone and Elsecar Owners' Company. The spin of a coin gave Silkstone the right to appear first in the title of the company which included Mrs Clarke, Earl Fitzwilliam, Lord Wharncliffe and the Wombwell Main Company.

These families were important in the development of early mining but the company was still small fry when compared to the large companies which dominated coal trade in the early part of the twentieth century, for the families' mines were too small to combat the opposition once the virgin coalfields in the Dearne Valley and Doncaster were exploited with the latest technology, the huge cost of which was beyond the means of small companies. Only the big boys survived in the twentieth century. It must be remembered that the families had elbowed smaller coal producers out of the way on their way up the mining ladder, another sign that only the largest and fittest survived in the industry, and that went for companies as well as miners on the coal faces.

Meanwhile, in the 1850s Barnsley was staking its claim to be the coal capital of South Yorkshire. With the coming of the railway in 1850 coal owners began sinking

shafts all over the town: 50 in that decade. In 1853 the Strafford Collieries, Stainborough, found the Flockton seam at a depth of 159 feet, in 1857 the Silkstone seam at 236 yards (five feet seven inches thick and all marketable coal), and in 1858 the Parkgate seam. This kind of operation was repeated all over Barnsley and the West Riding in that frantic decade: 374 pits in the riding produced nine million tons in 1855. While most mines were digging deeper to reach rich seams, some pits were working Silkstone seam coal a few yards below the ground: mines that would fit into your back garden. The Clarke family had worked, as well as large mines of course, the Little Pit (twenty yards) and Nopie (ten yards). There is an amusing story about Nopie Pit. Imagine the scene when a woman, Ann Paddle, fell down the ten yards-deep shaft. Luckily, she fell feet first and didn't suffer any injury. On being helped out she said she would not have cared a damn if she had not split her NEW wooden clogs! According to documents published at the time, there were twelve seams or beds in the Yorkshire coalfield, ranging from the New Hill, Abdy Coal and the Whinmoor (all two feet thick) and the Parkgate, Silkstone and Kent's Thin (five feet) to the prestigious Barnsley Bed (nine feet). Of these only the Barnsley Bed and Silkstone seams were said to be in quantities worth exporting. Barnsley also became a centre of trade and commerce, the railways drawing in shoppers from the neighbouring and newly established mining villages – on Wednesdays and Saturdays the town was said to double its population – as well as new industries to feed off the money supply generated

Above: Old workings at Elsecar, eighteenth or nineteenth century. The entrance to the workings can be seen near the Market Inn.
John Goodchild Collection, Wakefield.

by mining. But even in those days there were Jeremiahs. Just as today experts are always predicting that the earth's resources will run out, or that some plant or animal species is on the point of extinction, the experts in the 1860s were saying that the reserves of coal would be exhausted. Jevon's *The Coal Question*, published in 1865, warned that the nation could not continue its rate of progress because there would be no coal left. He said soon the mines would need to be 4,000 feet deep! By 1878, however, *The Standard* declared: "To a nation like England coal is only another name for gold, and we may even say that the presence of gold in Kent would be of far less importance to London than the existence of coal."

Between 1850 and 1880 Barnsley underwent extraordinary changes and much was due to mining and the underground savages, as miners were known. Barnsley had its old quarter, Market Hill, May Day Green and Shambles Street, each with a nearby labyrinth of yards, inns and crooked alleys but the rest of the centre had the look of a frontier town, the atmosphere of a frontier town without the gunsmoke. Early photographs show the facades of the shops had an impermanent

look as if the owners had hurriedly erected them on the grounds that the coal boom would not last and that they had to make a killing as quickly as possible. There was something transitory about Barnsley, a town in flux, all bustle, grime and excitement, and it was a rough town according to the local police chiefs with a reputation that went beyond the borders of the Yorkshire coalfield. Development was haphazard with pits and terraced streets appearing almost overnight: in the early days there was certainly money to be made and there was a general air of "stumbling vitality like a blind man on a spree," words which were also used to describe the wild and burgeoning mining towns of Wales. Whereas the frontier towns in America, Australia and South Africa had their wilderness a few hundred yards beyond the town boundaries, Barnsley had its "wilderness" hundreds of feet below ground in the honeycomb of galleries and tunnels where the conditions and environment were barren, hot and menacing. The core of this wilderness: the coal face where the miners hewed the coal and then shovelled it into tubs for transportation back to the shafts. To some miners the coal face was the "tigress," which was as fickle and as ferocious as

Above: Market Hill, the old quarter.

a wild animal and which claimed at least a life a week at most local pits; to some older miners the face was still controlled by primeval forces around which superstitions were spun.

Prosperity peaked in the early 1870s, during which it was thought prudent and fashionable to invest money in coal, a nice little earner for the owners of pit shares, as they would say today, and the coal owners, the big boys, came to the conclusion that sinking a shaft resulted in automatic riches. Coal was the new fuel needed for steamships, trains, factories and gas works and a new phrase became popular: "When you start working with coal, you soon stink of brass (money)." As in any age, fortunes were made and lost. Coal miners in some cases earned a pound a day – which earned them the nickname of gold miners, a phrase which would reappear in the national newspapers during the coal boom years of the 1970s, and they came to the conclusion that the wages spiral would never end and that the days of poverty were behind them. Appearing before a Select Committee in 1873, John Dixon, secretary of the West Yorkshire Miners Association, said many miners had been thrifty and had accumulated large bank accounts. Miners' homes were said to have "good chairs, china, bright brass candlesticks, chimney ornaments and mahogany chest of drawers." Like people today, miners expected their standard of living to rise each year and everyone declared with confidence that it was a new age, an age of full employment. Even the miners' union prospered,

Left: The market pictured in the 1890s. The market was an ancient institution long before the boom in coal.

Right: The miners' offices in Barnsley were designed to give the impression the union was a respectable organisation.

saving enough money to build the miners' offices in Huddersfield Road, an ostentatious and ornate building which demands attention. The design and construction were supposed to show to the outside world that the union was an institution as respectable as a bank or

Right and Below: Gillott coal cutting machines.

borough council, not a fly-by-night organisation like some of the other early unions: in many respects it was ahead of its time because the union was poised to hit the deck. As in modern property and share booms the coal mania ended in a big bang and by the mid 1870s and early 1880s the pits, the union and miners were on their knees. By 1880 few people wanted coal mines, the bottom having dropped out of the market. The owners and the miners, all bewildered by this sudden transformation in their fortunes, wondered what had happened to their world. Only the middle-aged and older men had known very hard times — in their nonage — and the younger men in the 1880s had not been programmed to handle such upheaval. In 1880 South Kirkby Colliery was offered for sale at the King's Head, Barnsley, but not a single offer was made; in 1882 Mitchell's Main Colliery, Wombwell, was offered for sale at the hotel but withdrawn at £2,000. Mitchell's was a new pit, opened in the 1870s in a blaze of publicity with the French tricolour flying from the pithead, one of the original backers being a French businessman.

Although coal mining was in the throes of a depression, at least one business connected with the industry was prospering. John Gillott and Son, of Summer Lane, are now largely forgotten but in the Victorian era their coal-cutting machines were ahead of their time. John Gillott, a former mechanical engineer to Newton Chambers and Company, of Thorncliffe, took out the first patent on the well-known Gillott and Copley machine in 1868. The patent consisted of a disc with cutting tools assembled on its circumference, driven by a pair of cylinders which oscillated. Later the machine was altered to the form which became in common use — two cylinders side by side. Mr Gillott did not claim to be the originator of the idea of a disc: his machine was an improvement on the machines of the type that

14

were then in use. The company was awarded a silver medal at a mining exhibition in 1885. By then John Gillott and Company were well established in Barnsley, at their Lancaster Works, the Dominion Works coming later. Both works, near the Summer Lane railway station, employed hundreds of men. The company prospered throughout the 1890s and by 1904 John's son, Joseph William, had bought the first car in Barnsley, a Norfolk, later owned by Eyre Bros.

In the 1890s, during which Barnsley settled down to become a carbon copy town with the banks, hotels and railway stations resembling their counterparts in other industrial towns in the north, the coal markets improved. The owners' resistance in the 1893 miners' strike collapsed when the demand for coal reached a new peak and the price went through the roof in London, the lucrative market for domestic as well as industrial coal. As a consequence new pits were sunk but the growth spots were Grimethorpe and the Dearne Valley rather than Barnsley and Silkstone. The first sod was cut at Grimethorpe Colliery on October 13, 1894, the "Barnsley Chronicle" reporting: "Instances are common enough hereabouts of sleepy, out-of-the-way villages being suddenly transformed into busy centres of population through the sinking of a new mine. Such a change, there is every reason to believe, will shortly be experienced in the village of Grimethorpe." One of the speakers, Mr C.G. Tyas, made a jocular reference to the fact that the best part of the Badsworth Hunt country had been taken by the mining company, and the runs some of them had enjoyed for so long would soon be impossible. Mr Joseph Mitchell, of Bolton Hall, who was the

managing director, said the new pit would be capable
of drawing 2,500 tons per day, more than one million
tons per year. As they got deeper with their sinkings,
more machines would become necessary and more
skilled men needed to work them, and he hoped that
miners would feel they had something more to do than
dog-racing and pigeon – racing. It was expected that
the Barnsley Seam would be reached at a depth of 500
yards and the total area of the new coalfield would be
3,000 acres, he said.

Grimethorpe was a sign of things to come. It was a
large colliery with massive reserves. The Doncaster
pits developed in the twentieth century – the titans of

the industry in Yorkshire – would resemble Grimethorpe
more than the small Barnsley pits sunk in the 1850s and
1860s and which had been seen as the pinnacle of
technological achievement in their day.

THE EARLY MINER

Coal mines – and miners – mushroomed in number
over a 20 year period. In 1837 pits in Silkstone and
Barnsley employed a total of 690 with another 100 at
Darton and Barugh, but with the sinking of mines like
Mount Osborne in Pontefract Road and Old Mill (1838)

COLLIERY OFFICIALS
AT TANKERSLEY COLLIERIES, NOVEMBER 1893.

and the opening of the railway in Barnsley in 1850, the flow of immigrants became a torrent and by 1858 there were 10,000 in the town.

Often wild and unpredictable the miners turned social conventions — and sartorial elegance — upside down. They sang in pit dialect, swore profusely, rioted and drank heavily: no wonder one observer "thought I was in a land of savages rather than in civilised England." While they lived, they lived riotously and while they worked, they worked resolutely. In 1842 it was said weavers sat pottering over their work for fifteen hours and spent one third of the time wishing it over; but colliers stripped and set to work as if they thought a pit was no place to loiter. Sometimes they worked recklessly with an arrogant disregard for safety, preferring to use naked lights rather than lamps.

The town had never seen anything like this tribe before and miners were a tribe, as tribal as the Mohicans or a religious sect: they had their own customs and code of conduct and as in all tribes the rules were designed to create a cohesive self protective group against the outside world. Sometimes there was a world within a world. At Carlton, Barnsley, there was a Welsh chapel where the hymns were sung in Welsh, the native tongue of many of the immigrant

miners who wanted to retain part of their heritage on moving to Carlton from South Wales. Irrespective of their social status or lack of it, outsiders were frowned upon and miners enjoyed showing that they were a race apart. Knocking the seven bells out of people they didn't like was one way of exhibiting their distaste for outsiders but when Barnsley miners were in a passive or jubilant mood they wore unconventional clothes as well. On Sundays and during holidays they discarded their pit clothes and dressed in gaudy attire, showy waistcoats called "posy vests" because of gaudy pictures of flowers on them, breeches fastened at the knees with stockings adorned with "clocks" and round hats which would be decorated with ribbons on special occasions. In *Memoirs of a Labour Leader* (published in 1910), John Wilson said the Durham miners in the mid-nineteenth century could be "identified by the peculiarities of their dress. Now that distinctive garb has gone." The adoption of such clothing was not only a symbol of their sub culture but a reaction against their oppressive underground working conditions where everything was Bible black except for the flicker of a candle or rudimentary lamp. It was said you could almost feel the darkness. Sunday was a day of rest, the day to let their hair down and they thought there was no better way to enjoy

Above: Colliery officials, Tankersley Collieries, 1893.
Yorkshire Mining Museum.

Above: Portrait of John Evans, 1819. He was buried without food or light for twelve days and nights in a mine near Wrexham. *The National Museum of Wales.*

pay day was a gathering ground for gamblers, drunks and fighters from neighbouring collieries. "Other collieries sent their contingent of men ready for any kind of mischief. To be like them was the peak of our youthful ambition." The Cornhill Magazine in 1862 found that young miners were "a rough, roystering, laughing, chattering, song-singing group" while their elders were "wildly intemperate or deeply religious." Describing a Yorkshire miners' gala in Barnsley in 1897, The Barnsley Independent declared: "The Yorkshire miner is outspoken in his criticism, as well as candid in his friendship. There was none of the scowling, murmuring discontent of the continental crowd about this gathering."

Few humans could have worked in such an underground environment without becoming brutalised, a fact that many of their critics, often middle class and strangers to the world of mining, failed to comprehend when they accused miners of all kinds of misdemeanours: newspapers were often full of their acrimonious scribblings which fed a gullible public with an anti miner diet without any deep analysis or defence from the miners. (As late as 1922 the Vicar of Silkstone, Rev. J. Prince, said while travelling in parts of England where there were no mines, he had felt the character of the miner was often misunderstood). To be fair to newspapers miners in the 1850s were still a relatively new breed, inarticulate as well as brutal, and society did not know how to cope with them and their strange ways and beliefs; society was frightened of the unknown and newspapers as usual reflected the opinions of the majority, the middle-of-the-roaders rather than an isolated and disliked minority. Many strange stories were told about this minority. Wilson, the Durham miners' leader, said there was a widespread belief in the 1840s and 1850s that miners lived as well as worked in the eternal darkness underground and that they were "little removed from barbarism." During the 1844 strike a Durham miner named Palmer went to London searching for work and was persuaded to visit a tavern where he was peered at and poked by the customers. Wilson wrote: "He was made to walk round showing his paces like a horse at a fair and the general cry was that he could walk as straight as other people; they thought pit men walked in a doubled-up posture owing to the cramped conditions of their work and their continual residence underground."

The miners' brutal side was not switched off when they had ascended the pit shaft of course and it manifested itself on the surface in their pastimes, including cock fighting, bare knuckle fighting to the finish, rat-baiting, matching dogs to a fight to a finish and in Wigan, for instance, in "purring," the rules of which stipulated that miners strip naked and then put on steel-capped clogs before clogging each other, a grisly and bloodthirsty pastime. In his History of Silkstone, and referring to the 1850s, the Rev. Prince said there were bare fist and clog fights in Silkstone (then a thriving pit community) and savage fights in the lanes between gangs of youths from different villages, all over something and nothing. Not all their games were brutal. The Edinburgh Review reported

themselves and forget about work than dress in clothes which contrasted with their drab attire underground. With a life expectancy of twenty-seven in the 1860s, miners thought life was too short to take anything too seriously.

The underworld in the mines influenced their style of clothes and seems to have shaped and hardened their characters as well, although gaudy pictures of flowers on waistcoats does not seem to fit the image of a robust miner! Brutality and coarseness were two features of their natures, more pronounced in the early miners than in most other humans, and in a way the features were mirror images of their working environment where nature was more brutal, more capricious and unforgiving than on the surface and where the gritty dust coarsened and toughened the skin and mind. "As a body they are animal, sensual and very ignorant," a writer stated in 1858. Two years later, however, J.M. Ludlow said he was "singularly struck with the clear heads, sharp words and thorough manliness of miners." John Wilson, born in 1837 and a future Durham MP, wrote in his autobiography that in 1863 that on Easter Mondays miners roamed round in gangs and claimed the right to heave, as they called it, every female whom they met. They lifted the women as high as they could and then saluted during their descent. However, the miners' treatment of pit ponies left much to be desired. Often glossed over in books, the treatment was so unsatisfactory as to require government intervention and legislation to protect the animals at the beginning of the twentieth century. For every ten men who treated their ponies as one would almost treat a pet animal, there was another who overworked or abused his animal.

To view the early miner through twentieth century spectacles is a mistake, for he was as different to modern man as a Scottish wildcat is to a domestic cat. To transport modern man back to the nineteenth century, a la Back to the Future, would be a traumatic experience because modern man would have difficulty in dealing with a world where the battle for survival was a daily ordeal and where strength, both mental and physical, was all important in miners' homes. Whereas modern man seeks a life as comfortable as possible, the old-fashioned miner had an aversion to anything that made the body soft and the modern world of labour saving devices and such things as after shave lotion and deodorants would have been treated with disdain by men whose ethos revolved around toughening their bodies to make sure they were in tip-top condition for work. Cuts, bruises, sprains and minor injuries were accepted without question as part of the job and no miner worth his salt would have used hot, rather than cold, water for what he called his morning swill.

Having a higher pain threshold than modern men seems to have been one of their attributes and doctors were seen as "not for the likes of us." Like other working people in those days, some never saw a doctor in their lives. There were two reasons why miners were reluctant to see a general practitioner — the cost and the fact that it was not seen to be manly to depend too much on them. The modern patient on average pays six visits per year to his doctor but for those tough characters six visits would have meant either a run of bad luck at work or a terminal illness! George Marsh, a miner born in 1834, who lived in the Penistone area and then moved to Pilley and whose recollections are available at Wombwell Library, did not see a doctor until he was sixty-four. "Since recovering from that illness I have not needed a doctor," he said at the age of seventy-seven, and "I can ride a horse with my boots on better than I could ride a mule when I was barefoot at seven." Not bad for a man who had walked barefoot to the mine when he was a youngster, who had begged barefoot and who did not have regular substantial meals until he was sixteen. (Marsh died in 1921). Edward Cowey, who became a president of the Yorkshire Miners' Association and who was known as a hard man, was born in 1839 and at the age of seven was working for fourteen hours per day sitting behind a trap door in the darkness. During a big miners' strike in the mid 1840s he tramped many miles over the Northern counties, barefooted and barelegged, to attend

Above: Pitmen playing quoits 1836, a painting by Henry Perlee Parker. *Loaned by the Laing Art Gallery, Tyne and Wear County Council Museums.*

meetings and hear the speeches of his relatives who were leading men in the union. Marsh and Cowey were not typical of course: many people died young and each family could expect at least one infant to die per generation; but it seems that if you were lucky enough to avoid the deadly childhood diseases and accidents at work, as well as the problems of middle-age, then nothing would stop you surviving into your nineties! In the end you just wore out.

Men born in the nineteenth century seem to belong to a different species. This was underlined when I saw the Channel 4 feature, *Adventure: The Logan Run*, screened in April, 1993, in which a modern team traced the footsteps of a 1925 expedition up Mount Logan, Yukon, Alaska, by sled. The programme showed the tenacity of the huskies and the bitter conditions the modern explorers had to endure; yet the leader of the modern expedition admitted that the pioneers, all of whom were born in the last century, had been in better mental shape and were more rugged than their modern counterparts, who had the benefits of science, the latest clothing for arctic conditions and substantial supplies of food via air drops. But the latest team had to rely on dogs to haul their sleds, whereas the original team had used their muscle power. The leader of the modern team paid tribute to the old team by saying that in the intervening seventy years modern man had

19

"lost" something when it came to surviving in harsh conditions. He said the pioneers, all of whom had reached the objective, had had such an arduous experience that few people recognised them on their return to civilisation in the 1920s. But they had stamina and managed to keep going, whereas only one member of the modern expedition, exhausted and stumbling, reached the mountain peak; the others fell by the wayside or were left to look after the dogs which were unable to work beyond a certain altitude. As I have said before the mining environment and a remoter uncharted characteristic which has since been diluted by progress shaped and toughened the early miners.

The nineteenth century industrial system also had an impact on them by encouraging the law of the jungle and therefore exaggerating the miners' worst features. The hours were long, the wages low and the system of weighing the coal, if it existed at all, was in favour of the employers, and the bitterness and distrust between employer and employees often exploded into open warfare with the miners having to rely on their rudimentary but often effective weapons, brawn and solidarity, to counteract the more sophisticated armoury of their adversaries who could rely on detachments of police or even the army when strikes got out of hand. The owners, who were alarmist and provocative, saw the Police as an extension of their coal companies; the miners were said to enjoy rioting. The 1850s and 1860s were turbulent times during which miners and coal owners engaged in frequent industrial combat, the survival of the fittest. The miners' reputation was at its lowest point at that time and yet there were forces at work which would change their persona in the long term: some of the forces had unexpected sources. It is assumed that the union was used by leaders and members as a battering ram with which to try to destroy the owners' economic might but the union also played its part in tempering the violent and disruptive influences in their lower ranks.

Some miners' leaders, even in modern times, have had more problems handling their own men than the so-called enemy. The "Yorkshire Post," reporting on a miners' demonstration in Sheffield in 1908, said the old miners' leaders could calm even the most rebellious of their members but at the latest demonstration there was real discontent at all three platforms and Mr. W. Crooks, MP for Woolwich, who was one of the speakers, could not persuade the audience to be quiet and he told one man: "I am 56, you don't look 30, but if you don't keep order I will punch your head." On the other hand the rank and file have enjoyed abusing and criticising their leaders: when Ben Pickard, general secretary of the Yorkshire Miners' Association and president of the Miners Federation of Great Britain, had his salary boosted to £500 per year, Joseph Knowles, the Hemingfield miner, wrote in his diary in the 1880s that miners were in uproar and would not contribute to make one of their own a prince (there is nothing new in mining: in the 1970s and 1980s some miners objected to the so-called lavish lifestyles of their leaders!).

With unions trying to convince society they were potentially respectable institutions and were not hell bent on revolution, the leaders probably found the violence and brutality of some of their members too much to stomach. The chapter on the unions and strikes in the nineteenth century has several references to leaders warning the men not to take the law into their own hands and one of the early unions, the Miners National Union, went out of its way to emphasise that it abhorred militancy. The leaders, mainly progressive men with a wider vision than their members, wanted to work inside the system and use the strike weapon as a legitimate last resort. Viewing themselves as a counterbalance to potential anarchy in the industry, the leaders turned the union into a kind of school, the unruly pupils of which would be educated and disciplined in the rules of the union in an attempt to keep the lid on the dissidents. That's not to say the leaders were appeasers, for they were prepared to take a tough line against mine owners when necessary. The leaders were in the main sincere and committed men who wished to improve the lot of their members, not just by putting money in their pockets – which was in short supply – but by improving them morally and spiritually as well, Victorian-style, and the leaders did much to calm down the violent and radical elements over many years. In the process they helped to grind down the early miners, change their ways, eliminate their dark and fierce sides.

Other influences which squeezed or knocked out the brutality and encouraged or enforced conformity and uniformity – and some would argue the miners' uniqueness as well – included the introduction of state education in the 1870s. D.H.Lawrence, the writer, always maintained that the first generation of miners' children to be educated at elementary schools were "beaten down" by the cane, both physically and in spirit. The church also played its part in this so-called humanization process: in the Sunday schools high-minded teachers were capable of putting the fear of God into underground savages by instilling into the children a new set of values and obedience. Today it is difficult to visualise the iron grip Sunday schools had on mining families, or any working class family, in the Victorian and Edwardian eras but generations of children were indoctrinated and disciplined by pious-minded men and women who believed they could improve the moral fibre of the nation. Society was changing at a whirlwind rate and with the growth of the state and the powers of local councils the populous were having to abide by more rules and regulations, at work, in the streets and at home. Conform or else was the order of the day.

The days of the early miners, bloody minded, undisciplined and often brutal, were numbered by the late 1870s. As with all men who have worked and lived too close to nature for too long, like farmers from another age, they were products of a raw environment more attuned to the crude laws of nature than to the laws of society. Their initial reactions came from the gut and muscles whereas other people's initial responses were often from the minds and consciences shaped by a society which had a different set of rules to colliers. Symbols of a society with which miners had no affinity, policemen were singled out for special treatment and law officers were reluctant to penetrate their close-knit communities, particularly on Saturday nights.

It is easy to denigrate the early miners, to concentrate on their flaws and vices but they had many redeeming features including the strength of

character and stamina to endure the underground hell, an extravagant and uncomplicated vitality for life and the strength to extract prodigious quantities of coal in the period before mechanisation made the job less arduous. They took on nature in savage combat, like mountain men on an untamed frontier, and faced death or injury every day. They were under valued by the coal owners, who believed pits ran themselves and who put a higher value on pit ponies than on miners. But despite all the flak from the owners and other stumbling blocks miners still managed to carry the industrialised world on their backs, to produce the coal for the factories, the steamships, the railways, the gas works and the middle classes, their fiercest critics.

As the second half of the nineteenth century came to its conclusion, most of the miners began to change. They discarded some of their brutal games, became more receptive to outside influences, less tribal; they reluctantly adopted a more conventional lifestyle and clothes. In the 1870s, the union tightened its grip on its members, and miners were told to be "respectably dressed" at miners' demonstrations. In a memo to branches the leaders said members should wear "a nice white rosette or a neat star, but by all means do not have a rosette the size of a dinner plate as we have seen at previous demonstrations (have nothing gaudy)." They were told to keep perfect order in the procession by walking four abreast, not to smoke and keep females out of the procession." In a speech at the opening of the new miners' offices in Huddersfield Road, Barnsley, in 1874, a union official outlined how miners' expectations were changing. Pointing the way to the future he said colliers would soon have pianos, cushioned chairs, carpeted rooms and "every variety of luxury which working men should possess as the producers of wealth." Although the changes did not take place overnight – the depression in the 1880s put paid to such luxuries for a time – a fundamental break with the past occurred in the 1870s and 1880s in respect to their values and expectations, as well as working conditions, and things would not be quite the same again. In 1910 Wilson, the Durham MP, wrote in his memoirs: "There have been wonderful changes in hours and conditions. It is worth something to look upon the changes and feel one has not been a drone in procuring the change." (Things had improved but by modern standards miners were still working in horrendous conditions in 1910).

Above: The shaft at Ardsley Oaks after the 1847 explosion.

UGLY PITS AND DISASTERS

Mines have never conjured up beautiful images and most writers have usually likened them to beasts or man-eating monsters. Emile Zola, the French writer describing the descent of miners into the shaft, wrote that "the pit gulped down mouthfuls of twenty or thirty men and did not seem to notice them going down." The pit cage resembling "some nocturnal beast, with its four decks each containing two tubs, leapt noiselessly up and down in the darkness." In *Sons and Lovers* D.H. Lawrence wrote that "one of the pits waved its plumes of white steam, coughed and rattled

hoarsely." Almost everything about a mine was seen as ugly and dehumanizing, from the spoil heaps (in *How Green Was My Valley* they were likened to the backs of monsters emerging out of the shaft) and the pit chimneys to the conditions the miners endured underground.

In one memorable but morbid passage in *How Green Was My Valley* the writer refers to peering at the "shining black strip in the orange light of the candles," believing it to be the "mourning band of the earth," and wondering whether they were committing an offence against nature... "and us taking it away to burn and she looking at us with half shut eyes, waiting for her reckoning." The author, Richard Llewellyn, said miners working underground were rarely free of the fear of the coal face; a mixture of nervous tension, claustrophobia and the darkness played tricks on the mind and sometimes they thought they could see faces in the shining coal, images created by the weak and distorted reflections of lamp light, and hear voices above the noise of the machines (*stories about the knockers*, the little spirits said to inhabit the mines, particularly in Wales, probably originated from such experiences). Jack Lawson, the ex-miner, MP and writer, had a different line of approach and did not mention beasts, saying instead that the bad and fickle moods of the pit were similar to those of a woman, "a she devil" who got her revenge in human lives: sometimes she was reluctant to let them go and the mine became the cemetery where miners were entombed.

These graphic but bleak descriptions of mines and life in the underground galleries illustrate the hazardous and almost barbarous nature of the job. Not only had miners to work in eternal darkness but they had to face water, gas explosions and falls of rock as well as inhale dust. Apart from sailors, miners in the nineteenth century had the most perilous jobs in the country. Accidents and explosions came in all shapes and sizes, sometimes involving one or two men, sometimes wiping out fathers, uncles and sons in the same family (men from the same family often worked together) and on rare instances killing most of the breadwinners in the same street. All explosions and accidents were horrific, some were bizarre. The Durham miner John Wilson mentioned one small explosion in which a miner was pushing a tub in which he had placed his picks. The blast hurled the miner into the tub, impaling him on a pick; it also removed another miner's finger-nails but left the rest of the body unscathed. Then there were the big explosions which could blow out the headgear, with flames and debris roaring up the shaft, often illuminating the night and attracting onlookers to the scene like moths to a light. The ground rumbled and the underground roof timbers collapsed like ninepins, and on the surface the noise of the falling roof sounded like the repeated firing of a distant artillery battery; if the wooden props withstood the blast and the flames they still became encrusted with cinders and soot, as did the bodies of the victims. Not only did the roof fall in, the floor was capable of rising when the earth moved as in the Barnburgh disaster, the pit tubs becoming embedded in the roof! No wonder pits were described as beasts and she devils.

The "she devils" had voracious appetites in Barnsley. Between 1841 and 1857 450 men and boys perished in firedamp explosions in Barnsley pits, said to be the most gassy and dangerous in Britain, and the figures did not include deaths from other accidents. The biggest disaster was at the Oaks Colliery in 1866 when 350 men and boys died. At Lundhill Colliery, Wombwell, nine years earlier, 189 men were killed in an explosion. About 200 men from both pits were entombed. The casualty lists from both disasters read like those in the local newspapers after the titanic battles of the First World War or a tragedy at sea. The mass funerals were on a scale never seen before in Barnsley. Victorian society was accustomed to unexpected death, for almost every family had experienced at least one case of infant mortality and cholera could wipe out all the inhabitants in a city slum street in a few days, but disease is as old as mankind and the working classes saw it as yet another cross to bear, a cross handed down from one generation to another. What happened in mining in Barnsley was different: the industry was still relatively new and when disaster struck it struck without warning and on a mass scale. It seemed, as in war, that the world was going mad, that there was no sense in all the carnage. Catastrophe followed catastrophe with perplexing and sickening regularity between the late 1830s and the 1870s: Husker, Mount Osborne (fourteen killed), Darley Main (seventy-five), Oaks (seventy-eight, 1847), Lundhill, Old Oaks and Swaithe (143, 1875) and it took time for science to come to terms with nature and produce the measures to make the underground scene as safe as possible. In addition, miners and management appeared to be incapable of becoming safety conscious, with men using naked lights rather than safety lamps because they provided better light and pit managers, some of whom in the early days could neither read nor write, turning a blind eye to certain perilous situations to try to produce more coal. It is difficult to visualise how unsophisticated miners were when it came to safety, but we have forgotten that since the Victorian era a new industry, complete with its own propaganda machine and its own way of doing things, has evolved to try to make people more safety conscious. Today all firms seem to have safety officers and posters festoon every office notice board. Back in the nineteenth century all workers appeared to be as bad as each other; for example during the construction of the Tay bridge men working on their small platforms attached to lofty positions on the superstructure would forget that below them were more men standing on similar platforms and hammers and other heavy tools repeatedly cascaded on to the lower levels, inflicting all kinds of injuries. Despite warnings from other workmen and management, the problem did not go away and careless workers continued to allow their tools to fall on workers who had to keep a watchful eye on the platforms above. Whereas the construction of a large bridge would involve the deaths of a few men, miners worked on the edge of a precarious world

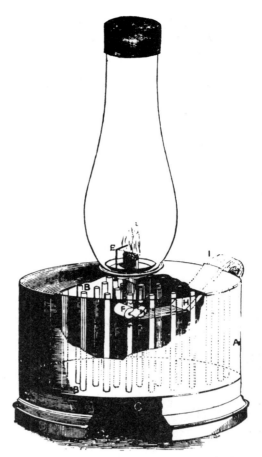

IMPROVED SAFETY-LAMP.

Left: This improved safety lamp was "safe and convenient" according to the Illustrated London News of 1848. The inventor said safety lamps had been used for many years but they were not absolutely safe under unusual circumstances. "The evils complained of in the modifications of the Davy Lamp are, that while they add to the security, they diminish so much the amount of light, as to render them practically useless." This lamp provided a superior light.

and human error underground or a quirk of nature sent them hurtling over the edge en mass. It was an ultra anxious and turbulent period during which families lived with the perpetual fear that fathers, sons, brothers and uncles would not return from the pit. The clatter of clogs in the back yard at the end of a shift was a reassuring sound to any family and all families felt uneasy when the father failed to arrive home on time.

The impact of a disaster on the early villages was more bewildering than on a pit village where several generations of miners had lived and worked, where disasters were part of the folklore and the perils and sorrow of mining were lodged in the social fabric. In the early pit villages many of the pitmen were new-comers to the industry as well as to the area and the indigenous population had no experience of having to deal with such horrific events in the community; no traditional outlets for releasing collective grief were in existence. The outlets came once the miners had set down roots, in the form of the strong bonds in the extended family, the camaraderie of the miners and the intimate social life of the twin props in mining communities, the chapel and the public house, all of which took decades to evolve and mature into effective release mechanisms but which later helped to spread the grief and relieve the tension during periods of abnormal adversity in the community. This is not to say that later mining families were hard or less likely to suffer grief or sorrow than other workers but the structure of the later communities, with the emphasis on social contact, good neighbours and

uncivilised manner. Once the national conscience had been troubled, however, there was no stopping the reformist zeal. A monument in Silkstone cemetery commemorates the disaster in which twenty-six children died in a flash flood. A very hot morning resulted in a violent thunderstorm in the afternoon with the stream running alongside the pit in Moorend Lane becoming a torrent which put out the surface furnace fires and made the Moorend Lane shaft inoperable. On attempting to escape via the old Husker (House Carr) drift and having negotiated the air doors, the children found themselves trapped against the doors as water broke into the drift. The water subsided quickly but claimed twenty-six children. Later they were buried in seven graves, the girls at the feet of the boys: the youngest was seven, the eldest seventeen. With public feeling running high, Queen Victoria sent a deputation to hold an inquiry into the mental and moral conditions in the pits. They found that women and girls wore trousers, worked naked to the waist and some women were expected to hew coal like men. Adolescent girls were employed alongside men who worked naked. After considering the report Parliament in 1842 banned the employment in mines of children under ten. The longest living survivor of the tragedy, Elizabeth Pashley, was still alive in 1903 and lived at the old cottages at Hillside, Silkstone.

Nearly 200 men and boys were killed at Lundhill on February 19, 1857, when a firedamp explosion ripped through the underground workings. Ninety women were widowed, 220 children orphaned and the Kellett family lost seven sons. Two hundred and fourteen men and boys descended the 660 feet deep shaft at the two year old colliery at six am. At twenty minutes past twelve a loud report and shock was heard and felt up to two miles from the mine. Writing in the "Barnsley Record," a reporter said he arrived at the colliery to find "the wild alarm, half-stifled enquiry and the almost maddened stare of the women and children at the pit-head baffled all description." On descending the pit a team of rescuers found they could not move in a southerly direction because the coal was on fire and therefore abandoned the operation, having realised their own lives were in danger. After the team left the pit a large volume of fire rushed to the mouth, the cupola becoming a mass of flames which illuminated the countryside. A stream had to be diverted to flood the galleries and the 185 bodies (four men were never traced) were not recovered for several months.

The Barnsley Record observed: "It will be remembered by many that the day preceding this explosion, February 18, was a dense, foggy day, with a lack of oxygen in the air. It is remarkable that previous disasters have been preceded by similar days." The writer recommended a "meteorological observance" to see if there was a connection. Today miners are still evacuated from a mine when there is a sudden and dramatic fall in atmospheric pressure which affects methane gas. The subsequent inquiry into the disaster declared there had been "criminal negligence, but the explosion was accidental."

"getting things off your chest" helped them to absorb and dissipate the emotional turmoil created by tragedy underground: they probably pioneered counselling without realising it!

It was one of the smaller disasters that changed the course of history. The 1838 Husker disaster at Silkstone brought to the public eye the working conditions experienced in mining communities. The fact that children were the victims touched the heart of a nation, and this was a nation which treated its young in an

Above: Lundhill Colliery, Wombwell, shortly after the disaster. Note the tourists. Today the site is a golf course.

Opposite: The London Illustrated News coverage of the Oaks disaster.

A year later a man was killed in a firedamp explosion at Wombwell Main Colliery, a mile from Lundhill. According to the H.M. Inspector's report, candles used by surveyors caused the accident and he wrote: "Soon after the Lundhill explosion, I advised the principal agent at Wombwell Main to abandon naked lights and adopt the use of safety lamps. I regret the suggestion was not acted upon. About seventy lamps had been introduced in certain parts of the mine but candles were permitted elsewhere. My belief is that the existing powers of the inspectors are not strong enough to subdue the reprehensible prejudice entertained by some employers (chiefly for economic reasons) against the use of the most efficient instrument yet for protecting their mining servants in the presence of gas." It was not just the fault of management. Conditions underground were primitive and men took risks. Although Davy lamps were invented in 1815 some miners still preferred candles because they provided a brighter light. Ventilation was poor, resulting in all kinds of ailments and not many miners worked beyond the age of forty or fifty. Until 1850 fatal accidents were not reported. The industry needed a shake-up, tough legislation and more inspectors.

Barnsley's worst mining disaster was the Oaks explosion in 1866, believed to have been Britain's largest peace-time disaster since the Fire of London.

It claimed the lives of more than 350 men and boys and forty pit ponies. The bodies of more than 100 men remain entombed to this day. The force of the early afternoon explosion on December 12 was such that the cage of number one shaft was damaged. Leased from Mr R. Micklethwaite of Ardsley, the pit was run by Messrs. Firth, Barber and Company and was sometimes called Ardsley Main. At the time 350 men and boys were underground and eighteen were found alive by a rescue team led by Mr T. Dymock, the managing director, who descended after hasty repairs to the cage. All the rescued men were badly affected by afterdamp and only six lived to the New Year. Later members of the rescue team, still underground, noticed that the air was being drawn from them into the lower part of the workings. The under-deputy, William Sugden, ascended the shaft to warn another party of men, led by Derby mining engineer, Parkin Jeffcock, of the danger. Ignoring the advice the second team, including Sugden, descended the shaft and then a second explosion ripped through the workings. The cage was sent down again but came back empty. Then a third explosion sent the cage roaring up the shaft into the headgear. To the astonishment and relief of the onlookers, one man had survived. Early the following morning the signal bell was heard, then a voice. With the cage and headgear out of action, a bottle of brandy and water was lowered on a piece

26

of wire. After a makeshift cage was made a youth called Embleton and a colliery official were lowered down the shaft. It was a courageous act for the pit winder baulked at the responsibility of his task. Drenched with water from burst water pipes they found Sam Brown sitting at the bottom of the shaft. The scene resembled hell with tubs of burning coal and the mangled bodies of the rescue team scattered in the roadways. Brown had been very lucky. The second explosion had knocked him unconscious and therefore missed the blast of the third. At last the Government Inspector decided that further journeys down the mine were too dangerous and he was proved right – a fourth explosion sent clouds of gas up the shaft the following day and there were further explosions over the next few days. The fire was eventually put out by stopping up the shafts to starve the flames of oxygen.

A year later there were still 260 bodies underground. About 160 were reclaimed over the next three years but more than 100 were never recovered. The inquest heard that the pit had one upcast shaft ventilated with a large furnace and two downcast shafts. Gunpowder was not used for blasting coal but had to be used to get through the hard stone underground. It was in use on the day of the first explosion. After a thirteen day hearing, the jury returned a verdict that Richard Hunt and others were killed by an explosion of firedamp but there was not sufficient evidence to

THREE HUNDRED AND FORTY-ONE
UNFORTUNATE SUFFERERS WHO WERE KILLED BY THE
DREADFUL EXPLOSIONS AT THE OAKS COLLIERY,
BARNSLEY, December 12th and 13th, 1866.

Opposite: There were discrepancies in the Oaks death toll figures. The Chronicle in 1867 referred to 341, the remembrance card to "upwards of 350" and a newspaper report ten years later stated 361. In 1966 the Chronicle mentioned 365.

prove where and how it was ignited. A second hearing, held in respect of the rescue workers, came to a similar conclusion but added that rescue parties should be limited in number and work in relays once it had been ascertained that there were no persons alive in the workings. It was decided to site the new Oaks Colliery half a mile away. The new pit — the junction into the old workings took place on the fourth anniversary of the explosion — saw naked lights banned and Clanny lamps and Stephenson lamps take their place.

There were further big explosions, including the Swaithe disaster in 1875 in which 143 men were killed (see *Pits 2*), but by the turn of the century tragedies involving large scale slaughter in Barnsley were almost over, safety having become the preoccupation of men, owners and government. Average death rates fell from more than four per thousand per annum around 1850 to 2.2 in the 1870s. But it was still a dangerous trade and almost every week the local newspapers carried stories with the headline "Fatal

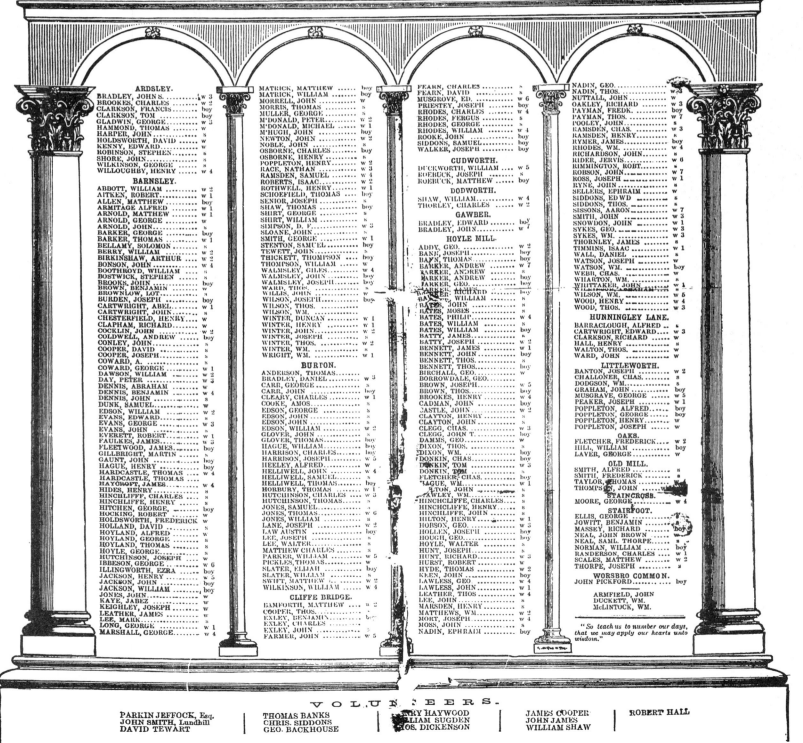

Presented Gratuitously to every Purchaser of the "BARNSLEY CHRONICLE," on Saturday, February 23rd.

accident at local pit." By the turn of the century roof falls had become the most common cause of death, although the occasional spectacular disaster still shook the nation: the worst was at Senghenydd in 1913 when 439 men lost their lives. In the peak years of the industry, between 1900 and 1913, one in ten workers in this country were employed in the mines and up to 1,000 were killed every year.

Stark statistics fail to illustrate the drama behind an accident. One of the most graphic descriptions of a pit mourning the death of a miner was written by Lewis Jones, a miner who had witnessed similar scenes on countless occasions: "The whole pit seemed to hold its breath, and the usual clamour was still. Yet as if the warm air had whispered the news in every ear, everyone knew what had happened in the pit, and in the pit bottom everything was in readiness" …On the day of the funeral: "…though the pit hooter blasted the air as usual, no one answered its hysterical screams. It kept blowing and bellowing like an animal robbed of its food, and still no one answered, until at last its shrieks faded and died out. The men had determined not to go to the pit on the day of the funeral."

THE STRIKES

The early miners' unions found it difficult to put down roots. The 1841 Miners' Association of Great Britain had fleeting success when it reached a membership of 100,000 but, like other fledgling unions, collapsed in the face of the power of the coal owners. The South Yorkshire Miners' Association was formed at a meeting at the White Bear in Shambles Street, Barnsley, in April, 1858, when delegates agreed to set up branches. Membership fluctuated and by the mid-1860s the association had 2,000 members in eighteen lodges. In 1872 John Normansell, general secretary of the South Yorkshire miners, was the first miner to be elected on to a local authority, Barnsley Borough Council. At the 1873 miners' demonstration in Wakefield men carried sixty banners, many of which were nine feet by seven feet and made of pure silk, a sign that miners and the union − in this case the West Yorkshire Miners' Association − were becoming prosperous. About 30,000 were said to be present at the demonstration. By 1874 the South Yorkshire association and the North Derbyshire Union had substantial memberships and money in the bank which enabled them to open new offices in Huddersfield Road. In 1877 the demonstration at Pontefract was said to be a mere shadow of those organised between 1872 and 1874. In 1875 there had been forty seven brass bands but two years later the number had dropped and only 8,000 people assembled in the park.

In 1880 only 2,800 out of the 60,000 Yorkshire miners were organised and union funds had dwindled from £50,000 in 1876 to about £6,000. According to the former Barnsley journalist, Harold Bunting, writing in the "Sheffield Mail" in 1926, strikes in the 1870s and 1880s were sometimes declared by the men without consultation with the union leaders. In September 1879 a strike started at Monk Bretton Colliery which drained £1,500 from the association's funds. It lasted nearly 12 months. Such strikes, coupled with bad times, led to men drifting away from the union and in 1881 the South Yorkshire Association and the West Yorkshire Association merged. The year 1889 saw the formation of the Miners' Federation of Great Britain,

Below: The Oaks memorial to the Oaks rescue team erected in 1913. See page 139.

The Remembrance Card

In Remembrance of the
UNFORTUNATE SUFFERERS,
WHO
LOST THEIR LIVES
IN THE OAKS COLLIERY EXPLOSION,
BARNSLEY,
DECEMBER 12, 1866,
WHEN UPWARDS OF
350 Souls were Launched into Eternity.

The Angel of Death spread his wings on the blast,
  And the eyes of the sleepers wax'd deadly and chill,
In the face of the miner he breathed as he pass'd ;
  And their hearts but once heav'd, and for ever grew still.

"Prepare to meet thy God."

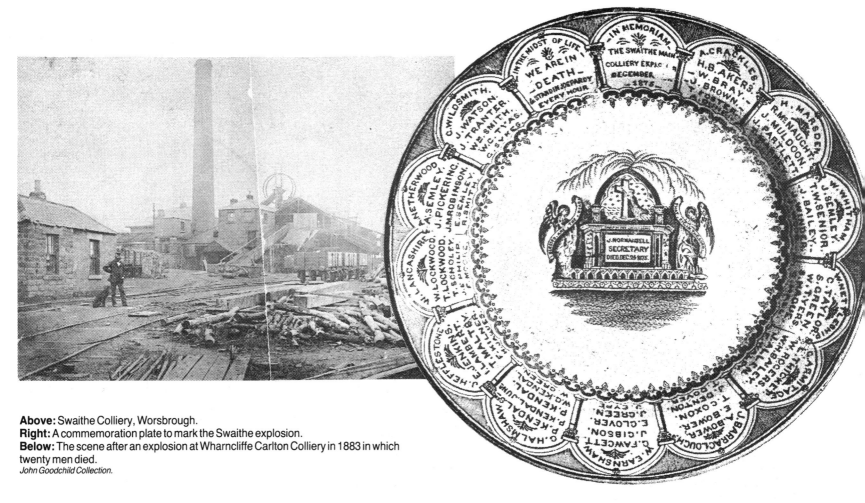

Above: Swaithe Colliery, Worsbrough.
Right: A commemoration plate to mark the Swaithe explosion.
Below: The scene after an explosion at Wharncliffe Carlton Colliery in 1883 in which twenty men died.
John Goodchild Collection.

Right: The Thorncliffe riots of January, 1870 stemmed from a lock-out by the colliery masters Messrs. Newton Chambers Co. In March of the previous year the owners served notice on their miners after "interference" by the South Yorkshire Miners' Union in their affairs. Homes of non-union workers at Westfield Row were attacked by a mob and broken into. Household goods were stolen by the rioters, 29 were arrested and brought to trial. Twenty four of the men were from Barnsley and worked at Tankersley Pit. The illustrations show the prisoners being escorted to the courthouse at Barnsley and the scene in the court.

ESCORTING PRISONERS TO THE COURTHOUSE AT BARNSLEY

covering all the inland coalfields and by 1899, Scotland and South Wales. By 1893 the federation had 300,000 members. Yet by 1900 only two thirds of the national workforce had been unionised. Membership had a tendency to rise when coal markets were robust and contract during slumps or depressions when the coal owners had the upper hand. On top of that hewers in the last century were basically self employed men who displayed all the attributes and flaws of such men: an independent frame of mind and a streak of bloody-mindedness; they did not like being regimentated.

Some of the strikes in the nineteenth century left behind a trail of violence, evictions and hard poverty. The 1864 dispute was a good example. The stoppage started early in the year when the Coal Masters' Association closed Oaks, High Royd and other pits until the Oaks miners' demand for a wage rise was withdrawn. About 560 were members of the union and 3,000 non-union. At a meeting of the Barnsley Guardians, Mr U. Corbett, one of the Inspectors said that miners with a wife and children would have to go into the workhouse when they ran out of money. On April 21 a meeting was held on May Day Green, attended by a large group of miners. According to "The Barnsley Record" "Cheapside presented an animated appearance. A large number of miners with their wives and children then made off to the workhouse, where a number of policemen were on duty to prevent anyone going in save those who had orders." In May the Masters' Association opened Oaks and High Royd pits to allow miners who wanted to work to return at the old rates. After a union meeting was held to warn miners not to go back, the Record reported that miners

who broke the law by attacking "black sheep" (black legs) would not receive a penny from the union. A Mr W. Cartwright, stated the newspaper, said all the miners had seen what the union could do and he hoped that if they ever resumed work, they would join the union and pay to it like men. A Mr George Moore said he knew plenty of men who had worked at the Oaks Colliery for three shillings a day, a low figure.

There was a whiff of gunpowder in the air three days later when "a good deal of excitement was created in Barnsley by the arrival in the centre of some hundreds of colliers with a cart pulled by men." The cart contained a number of Oaks workmen with printed notices in their hats. It appeared that the men had been given notice to quit their colliery houses that afternoon, when "there had been scenes of

Above: Believed to be the start of the Barrow Miners' gala procession, assembling at Worsbrough Bridge, about 1890. *South Yorkshire County Record Office.*

Below: Yorkshire Miners' Offices.

Above: Police were drafted into Barnsley during the 1893 dispute. Pit officials and East Riding Police pictured at Woolley Colliery.

violence and riot." The tension turned to farce in July when Hannah Goodliffe and Mary Haigh appeared in court charged with assaulting Mr Thomas Ashirst and causing damage to his property to the amount of two shillings and sixpence. Walking to work Mr Ashirst said he was followed by a number of children who escorted him by playing tin cans. When a lad called Goodliffe threw a stone at him, he seized the boy and took him to the complainant's house. Ashirst had not been at home long when Mrs Goodliffe arrived and demanded the return of her son. Mrs Goodliffe must have been a formidable woman, for she struck Ashirst and then threw stones at his windows. Mrs Haigh, the other defendant, was a little more direct — she broke down the door with a firm kick. She was fined five shillings and Mrs Goodliffe 10s. The lad was ordered to be kept on bread and water for twenty-four hours.

On arriving in Barnsley in a cart on a shopping expedition, escorted by policemen, on July 16, the wives of six "black sheep" found themselves facing a large crowd shouting "Baa, baa blacksheep." The women went to a flour store and two grocery stores in Sheffield Road, but the traders, threatened by the crowd, refused to sell them anything. As the crowd became more threatening one of the workers' wives fainted several times. On the return journey along Doncaster Road the inhabitants turned out with frying pans, shovels and set-pot covers which they beat all the way to the Oaks Colliery. Throughout the day and

night large crowds assembled outside the pit and as the workers came out they were shouted at, and those who lived in Barnsley were escorted home by the police or chased by the mob. One man escorted to his home in New Street had to face the gauntlet of onlookers drumming tin cans and shouting.

At a meeting of miners, Mr. Normansell, the chairman, said men at the High Royd Colliery had not received an increase in pay for eight years, although the price of coal had increased by two shillings and sixpence a ton during the same period. One man at the meeting claimed the owners at Silkstone had loaded a table with roast beef, pudding and other delicacies, and then sat down to eat it in the presence of starving miners. On July 25 the owners decided to end the lock-out, sending out circulars to customers announcing their intention to resume work in a few days. The men eventually drifted back to work at the old rates.

Victory followed defeat, in 1866, when miners at Edmunds Main and Swaithe Main achieved a five per cent rise in their wages as a result of a strike. This prompted the editor of the Record to declare: "A time has come when trade unions must be taken notice of, attended to with proper respect when right and put down when wrong. The association of miners are strong and growing stronger every day, and the Association of Masters should be in the same position."

COLLIERY OFFICIALS
WEST RIDING AND CHESHIRE CONSTABULARIES
at Wharncliffe Silkstone Colliery, South Yorkshire,
DURING COAL STRIKE, OCTOBER 2nd 189?

The 1870s and 1880s were riddled with disputes but none could compare with the 1893 lock-out during which youths roamed the outskirts of the town demanding tolls and mobs wrecked pit premises. Such was the violence that the authorities were compelled to call in the army — about 200 soldiers — and an extra 300 policemen from the East Riding, Cheshire and London. Having refused to accept a twenty-five per cent reduction in wages, the Miners Federation of Great Britain found their members were locked-out in July. Within five weeks the iron trade was suspended in some parts of the country and the price of coal began to rise, a significant development which resulted in the owners' resolve cracking a few months later. Trouble must have been brewing when Mr Ben Pickard, MP, and president of the Miners Federation, said in September that any miner causing a disturbance outside the law would be a traitor to his cause. Four days later, when some men lodging in Heelis Street were suspected of working at Barrow Colliery, a nasty incident occurred. After the men had entered the Shoulder of Mutton pub a crowd gathered

outside and then hurled stones and other missiles through the windows. The balloon went up the following day when 400 young men descended on Rylands Colliery, Stairfoot, and smashed windows. With rumours spreading that men were working at Mitchell's Main, Wombwell, a large crowd gathered on the canal bridge leading to the pit; some deputies who were working at the pit were treated roughly and the police were called. Down the road 2,000 people met in the market place at Wombwell, the speakers demanding that men be withdrawn from Mitchell's and that work cease on a stack at Hoyland Silkstone pit, Platts Common. Marching to Hoyland, 700 men descended on Hoyland Silkstone from four directions, forcing labourers to flee the pit yard. Struck by a cudgel, the pit manager had to be protected from further injury by some of his workmen. To round-off the visit someone blew a whistle and stones, bricks and bolts were hurled at the premises. Rockingham Colliery at Hoyland Common was the next target. On the way the men met a drayman with a load of ginger beer. "Entering into the humour of the situation,"

Above: West Riding and Cheshire Police and pit officials at Wharncliffe Silkstone Colliery, Tankersley.

35

OFFICIALS CHESHIRE AND WEST RIDING CONSTABULARIES ON DUTY AT TANKERSLEY COLLIERIES, DURING THE GREAT COAL STRIKE, OCTOBER 25th, 1893.

Above: Police and officials at Tankersley Pits.
Yorkshire Mining Museum.

according to the *Barnsley Chronicle*, the drayman said they were welcome to all he had provided they did not smash the bottles. At Rockingham the premises were wrecked and the stables burned down. Assuming that they would be the next target, management at Barrow Colliery telegraphed for more policemen and when the mob saw one of the newly arrived policemen they changed direction, heading towards Blacker Hill. Marching past Hoyland Silkstone Colliery, now in the hands of the police, the mob moved on to Elsecar and headed for Simon Wood Colliery in front of Reform Row, where policemen on the canal bank were pelted with stones. At Hemingfield pit, five minutes walk from Simon Wood, the strikers amused themselves by pushing pit tubs down an incline; then they pushed each other into the canal! Returning to Simon Wood they destroyed a cabin and 500 miners' lamps.

It was too much for the authorities to stomach. On September 6 a detachment of between fifty and sixty men of the 6th Dragoons came to the town from York, to be followed by the Dublin Fusiliers who were stationed at Wombwell Main Colliery. Also drafted in were 100 men from the Royal Scots and 300 policemen.

Meanwhile, gangs were roaming the roads demanding tolls. Faced with men armed with sticks, Mr J. Kaye, a JP, and a police superintendent who were in a hansom cab near Hoyland paid their toll. One gang moved into New England, Worsbrough, but the local residents formed a vigilante group and drove them off in the direction of Birdwell. Mr John Frith, a union official, said he did not think members of the Yorkshire Miners Association were involved. With authority breaking down, the Mayor of Barnsley warned that riots and disturbances would be quelled by the police and army. As 100 men from the Suffolk Regiment arrived, traders distributed soup and provisions to the needy but the *Barnsley Chronicle* declared: "Unfortunately, many who obtained relief were not connected with the stoppage." The trouble quickly subsided and the *Chronicle* stated that between September 9 and 16 the town was quiet, with miners' lodges meeting and condemning the violence.

With the approach of winter, coal picking operations were stepped up, one of the favourite sites being Providence Main, a quarry hole belonging to Clarkson's Old Brewery. In their makeshift mines

Above: A soup kitchen in the 1893 dispute. The landlady and landlord at The Cock Inn, Birdwell, gave miners breakfast.
Loaned by K. and Mrs Burkinshaw, Birdwell.

Left: Darton Cyclists' Club who attended a fancy dress parade at Ravensthorpe in aid of the miners' soup kitchens, September 1893. The photograph was taken outside the Rose and Crown, Darton. *Loaned by Mrs E. Thompson, Darton*

DARTON CYCLISTS' CLUB AS NEGROES
Cyclists' Fancy Costume Parade at Ravensthorpe,
IN AID OF THE
MINERS' SOUP KITCHEN
DURING COAL STRIKE, SEPT. 24th, 1893.

colliers dug deeper and deeper and there were fears someone would be killed if the roof or the sides of the shafts collapsed.

This occurred at the disused Mount Osborne pit in Pontefract Road where Arthur Dodson, aged 41, died when the sides of his eight ft. deep shaft collapsed around him.

Meanwhile, the miners' long struggle began to pay off. The nation was crying out for coal and the dispute was settled on November 17, the men returning to work at the old rates. The *Daily Chronicle* declared: "A triumph of labour such as the world has never seen. All along the line they (the miners) have stood firm through the weary months. Their discipline and loyalty, their sublime endurance, their faith in one another are as unshakable today as they were at first." The dispute, involving 300,000 workers in the central coalfields, was the most widespread miners' strike in the nineteenth century. It proved that united action could produce results and paved the way for the successful 1912 minimum wage strike, the first to involve all the coalfields.

A RACE APART

As the nineteenth century progressed miners grew in numbers and virtually took over erstwhile farming villages; at best they were regarded as different by the rest of the inhabitants, at worst they were seen by their so-called betters as a swollen and threatening underclass. Much of the problem was due to people's preoccupation with status in the rigid class-ridden Victorian society where men who worked underground like animals were bound to be seen as inferior. On the other hand miners often regarded themselves as special and viewed other people as inferior. Their inverted snobbery was based not on status, money or academic success but on muscular power, their own mark of distinction, and on their ability to cope with adversity underground.

Miners' relationships with other workers and classes can be examined by tracing the history of a local mining town, like Wombwell, which underwent a transformation in the nineteenth century. Wombwell was a picturesque village, similar in appearance to one of Hollywood's olde worlde studio backdrops — without the frills — but within decades of the sinking of the first shafts at Lundhill in 1853 that old world had vanished. It was a typical Victorian story: a village steeped in its pastoral stability and stifling backwardness was pitchforked into a crude, constantly changing and lively town where the predominant features were chimneys, spoil heaps, dirt, noise and people: the antithesis of village life.

In 1851 the population (including Hemingfield and Jump) was 1,627, almost the same figure as in 1839 when the census returns revealed 803 in Wombwell, 346 in Hemingfield and "20 in canal barges." There was still a Lord of the Manor, a squire (Garland), seventeen farmers, two blacksmiths, three butchers, three maltsters, seven shoe-makers, three tailors, two masons, one brick-maker and a scythemaker. By the 1860s primitive pithead gear and long ribbons of black pit chimney smoke, sometimes stretching for nearly two miles across the sky, were beginning to appear and Wombwell had become half mining, half pastoral, the population having risen to 3,758, with most of the miners living in rows of houses near or attached to the new mines, all of which were on the boundaries of the village. According to a Government Inspector, Lundhill, Broomhill, Low Valley, Tingle Bridge, Smithley, Wombwell Junction, Wombwell Main, Hemingfield, New Jump and Wood Head "were more or less centres of population, there being coal mines or other works at all these places."

All the pit communities were virtually self-contained — at Lundhill, for instance, there was a chapel and public house — and contact with the rest of the community was sporadic. Mr F Machin, in his *History of the Yorkshire Miners*, said it was not unusual for miners in the county to live in "villages away from other workers and out of sight of the rest of the community." By 1865 Wombwell could not cope with the rising population: in ten years the number of cottages almost trebled to 644 "with two or three families crowded into one cottage," according to the government report at that time. With most people having to depend on shallow wells the water supply was inadequate and there was a bad case of fever at New Jump Colliery, thirty cases being reported in four houses in 1864. Despite the new pits and houses on the outskirts there had not been many changes elsewhere, particularly in the main street which consisted of a straggling line of ancient farmsteads, orchards, huddles of grey farm-workers' cottages and a small mining community in Alma Street, which appeared incongruous in that otherwise rural scene. There was resistance to change. Many of the farmers and farm-workers' families had lived in Wombwell for generations in their own rustic isolation, immersed in their own way of life and beliefs in what was beautiful and rich countryside: it was a community proud of its close-knit spirit and the quantity and quality of its grain, just as future generations of miners would be proud of their community spirit and the quality and quantity of the coal. The farm-workers' way of life had remained unchanged for generations — visitors in the 1860s would have seen the scythe and sickle in use in the fields — and even the opening of the canal at the beginning of the nineteenth century had caused but a few ripples in the slumbering community.

It was industrialisation that knocked out nature and ended peaceful seclusion, bringing in its wake all the horrors and dazzling trinkets of the new world. The new mines, deeper and more productive than the older mines in Barnsley, were seen to outsiders as ugly monsters that devoured men and disgorged mountains of spoil, and the farmers and their workers, fearing change, did not take too kindly to the immigrants, the black-faced stormtroopers of the new industrial age who had strange beliefs and who despoiled the earth and the air.

The two camps kept each other at arm's length, although they were quite similar in many respects.

Like miners, farm-workers were not noted for their sharp wit, were proud of their strength and often boasted they had not suffered from a headache in their lives! They probably had their own wild men as well, a minority who were as much an embarrassment to the rest of the farming clan as the brutal miners were to their moderate contemporaries. Flora Thompson, the writer who chronicled life in Oxfordshire villages in the 1880s, blamed too much inter-marriage for the riotous life in her villages and it is not unreasonable to assume there was a similar faction in Wombwell, which had slept for centuries without any outside influences. Like miners, farm-workers regarded strangers as enemies, the result of "hanging around in clans," according to Thompson. Old farm-workers, like old miners, were physical wrecks with gnarled or swollen hands: they walked home like cripples "stiffly stalking along, leaning on sticks" (Thompson). Long hours on the land in all kinds of weather had left their mark on the farm-workers. Towards the end of the century crippled old farm-workers became a rare sight; however, they were replaced by equally old miners who had an infirmity all of their own — pneumoconiosis (miners' lung disability caused by dust: it affected the breathing and put added strain on the heart).

Although most of the indigenous population regarded miners as interlopers or enemies, some welcomed them with open arms. Traders and landowners saw new opportunities, new horizons. In 1798 there had been ten landowners in Wombwell, six of them absentee. With the sinking of the pits some sold their land for speculative building and then moved their money out of the area, thus beginning a tradition which has cursed mining areas ever since: profits from mining and associated industries have been rarely ploughed back into mining areas and this has left places like Wombwell and Barnsley with the second best when it comes to the environment and housing.

In the 1870s and 1880s there was large scale house building (1870 saw public lighting by gas) and by the late '80s new shops, large by the standards of village life and mainly built by the Co-op., were appearing, one of the first being at the bottom of Melville Street, a blockhouse of a building which reflected the growing prosperity and influence of the Co-op. as well as being a clear sign that mining was no longer a passing phase and was here to stay. But much of the old character of the village was still intact. The farmsteads and stone cottages were still prominent features and there was a distinct cultural demarcation line between the farms and the mining communities, with the few shop-keepers and artisans somewhere in between. Although miners were now in the majority — in 1871 only one in ten workers was employed in agriculture — they were still at the bottom of the social pile and even the poorest farm-worker would feel superior to the large mining families who lived in overcrowded conditions.

The old village could not last forever, however, for change was coming at a whirlwind pace and as the workers flooded in more rows of terraced streets were

built, more substantial than the earlier properties (there had been one up, one down houses in earlier times) and between the 1880s and 1910 the streets fanned out from the main street to meet the collieries and their communities expanding in the opposite direction. It was a boom town. In 1899 the second railway station — Wombwell West — opened and by 1910 there were 13,000 people in what had become a township or townlet with its own urban council and town hall. In fifty years the population had risen by nearly 12,000; in the previous half century by a few hundred. The three Wombwell pits employed large numbers of men (Mitchell Main, for instance, had more than 2,000 on the books) and were exporting more than 300,000 tons of coal per year, a peak figure. The farmers and farm-workers were being elbowed out of the way, becoming a tolerated but awkward minority, a far cry from the 1850s when they dominated the scene. The town was a new cultural melting pot which drew immigrants from Staffordshire, Lincolnshire, the

Above: High Street, Wombwell, circa 1910. The Co-op building is on the left.

North East and Leicestershire, almost all of whom were connected with mining.

Miners in the pre-1914 period comprised three quarters of the working population in Wombwell, a very high figure when one considers that even at the height of the nineteenth century mining families were fewer than a third of the population of the coalfield areas. But there still seemed to be a discernible gap between them and the rest of the community, as Joe Hall later points out in this chapter. That there was a gap should not be surprising because employees of mining companies have never formed a cohesive group; in fact, the rigid hierarchy existing underground manifested itself on the surface in the housing conditions and social life. The hierarchy — pit management, deputies and miners — had three distinctly different types of houses, all suitably furnished to extol the inhabitants' status, if any, and each group of houses was segregated from the others to avoid social contamination. The managers had the best houses, of course, and the pit deputies houses which had a front door leading into a corridor and not straight into the living quarters as in the miners' houses. Even the miners' houses were split into sub categories. The higher paid miners, the hewers, could afford to pay for reasonable housing — but still inferior to that of managers and deputies — and the lower paid miners lived in cheap high density housing which acquired notorious nicknames in Wombwell such as "flying poker row" (an allusion to frequent domestic rows) and "three-cornered hell," three rows of houses at The Guide Post where life was said to be akin to the slaughter on the Western Front. With such divisions in the mining world, between management and deputies, deputies and miners, and even hewers and other pit workers, it is not surprising that miners never had the inclination to form social bridges with workers in other industries and trades. When it came to work and strength miners always felt they were a little superior to the rest.

A future miners' leader, Joe Hall, born in Lundhill in 1887, one of eleven children (the boys slept at one end of the bed, the girls at the other), always blamed other sections of society for the miners' isolation. He often spoke of miners being treated as an underclass before the turn of the century. Reflecting on his life more than thirty years ago, Joe told a Sheffield journalist: "We were untouchables, underground savages. A miner's daughter had little chance but to marry other than a miner. The miner had no choice but his own."

But there were other reasons for this "them" and "us" attitude. Their work was different, underground instead of on the surface, and outsiders would view men who worked in such conditions, hundreds of feet below the surface and who emerged looking like negroes as socially inferior. They also had a reputation for hard drinking and violence and so-called respectable people would keep them at a distance. Early miners, like all primitive people, had their beliefs and superstitions. Widespread in coalfields and probably incomprehensible to other people at the time, these superstitions illustrated the gap in the mentality between miners and other people. They survived for a number of generations, well into the twentieth century in one instance — that miners who saw a woman on the way to work would return home believing that it was a bad omen. Some of the superstitions are interesting and whoever instigated them had it in for women and birds. A pit manager wrote in the 1870s: "I know one man who would not go down the shaft if he saw a white pigeon on his way to work, believing that an accident would occur to him. If miners saw a white bird hovering above the head-gear they believed an explosion of foul air was imminent." In 1902, when one was seen above the head-gear at a pit in Wales, 300 miners went on strike. A year earlier the "South Wales Weekly News" reported that an explosion at a local mine was blamed by some miners on a robin which had made a nest in the pump-house. Whistling down a mine was supposed to be unlucky and was said to upset the knockers, whose spirits were said to inhabit the mines (see *Pits 2*). In the North East fathers and sons would not descend the shaft in the same cage, in case the ropes broke. These superstitions developed at a time when scientists were baffled by the causes of underground explosions and other accidents and lesser mortals, convinced that their destiny rested with the gods or something primeval, came up with their own theories and conclusions. In a cynical age, like the 1990s, it is easy to believe that someone may have enjoyed kidding people and that a miner who did not want to go to work could easily come up with some bizarre excuse to con the gullible manager. But you have to remember your own family's old superstitions; in my case superstitions relating to thunderstorms — that mirrors and silver knives and forks had to be covered in case they attracted lightning — to realise that people, like my grandmother, who were born in the last century had minds shaped by different experiences and thoughts, that they accepted their parents' beliefs without question and that their irrational fears were real to them.

Mining has always been a dangerous occupation and as a consequence miners believed they did not have to conform as much as other people. Again miners thought they were special. According to a contributor in the *Barnsley Chronicle* in 1933, miners in the 1850s and 1860s "looked upon themselves, by reason of the hardships they endure, to immunities to which other men should accord them." The miners expected "undisturbed quarters, respectful distances and freedom from arrest." A policeman rarely showed his face among them. "It was no pleasant thing to walk through a primitive mining village when miners were on the high road," he wrote. This was a fairly accurate snapshot of life at that time — although it would be useful if the writer's background was known, since the middle classes often painted a black picture of miners without any analysis — but by the First World War it was an anachronism. Miners had moved on and were living typical working class lives, yet the middle classes retained in their minds that old image (coal in the bath, etc) of miners well into the 1930s, probably because it was easier for them to deal in

Left: The last building in the former mining hamlet of Lundhill — Lundhill Tavern.
Scott Bairstow, Barnsley Chronicle

stereotypes and cliches than in reality. The writer, George Orwell, recalled a cartoon in *Punch* at the end of the First World War: miners were earning high wages and certain factions in society were worried that they would soon be living beyond their station in life. The cartoon portrayed three sinister miners in a new, cheap car. A passer-by asks: "Have you borrowed that car?" "No, we have not borrowed it — we have bought it," came the reply. The fact that miners, inferior people, could afford to buy a car, a symbol of middle-class life, was a bitter pill to swallow. The message was quite clear — give the miners money and they would soon be buying and taking other things that really belonged to the chattering classes. Their worst fears did not materialise. In reality, once the post war boom was over, many miners ended up on poverty row in the 1920s.

The miners' role in society and their relationship with other classes is fascinating, and this article has merely brushed the subject. In a way that separateness has never gone away. During the 1984 miners' strike Mrs Thatcher referred to the "enemy within," an arcane and archaic comment about miners, reminiscent of Winston Churchill in the 1920s when he described miners as "the enemy." It was robust and threatening language, the kind usually reserved for IRA bombers or other terrorists, not ordinary people.

MAP OF THE
BRITISH COALFIELDS.

Exposed Coalfields.
Supposed concealed Coalfields

Scale of English Statute Miles.
10 5 0 10 20 30 40 50

Chapter 2

1900-1920 Boom and War

Below: Yorkshire Miners galas in the early years of the century. The banner in the bottom photograph is Wharncliffe Woodmoor.
Loaned by R.D. Watson, Darton

Between 1900 and 1914 Barnsley firmly established its reputation as the coal centre of South Yorkshire. After the 1912 minimum wage strike a coal boom was sustained until the beginning of the First World War in August, 1914. In January, 1914, the *Barnsley Chronicle* declared: "The past year has been remarkable, not only for the volume of business but for the high prices. On the other hand working costs and wages have never been higher, the men enjoying a minimum wage. Costs have increased owing to the fact that the miners have not been prepared to toil the whole available working time when they have made a satisfactory wage in a smaller number of days. Yet, with all these extra costs, the colliery owners have enjoyed a prosperous year."

Although Barnsley could still boast that it was the principal coal town of South Yorkshire, there were the first signs that it would be knocked off the pedestal in the 1930s. Developing the virgin area between Rotherham and Doncaster, where new pits were being laid out, coal owners were predicting in 1914 that these pits would produce a million tons per year. Mr J. Hewitt, president of the Barnsley and District Coal Owners Association, speaking at a meeting in February of that year complained that some Doncaster pits were producing coal below the Barnsley price. After suggesting that the new Doncaster pits pay a higher minimum wage to relieve the pressure on Barnsley, where the pits were generally smaller and the seams thinner, he said Barnsley was still the centre of the best quality coal in Yorkshire but warned that the industry was vulnerable to trade cycles.

At that time exports were booming. South Yorkshire pits sent more than seven million tons to Hull between 1913 and 1914, northern Russia, the biggest customer, importing one million, an increase of 200,000 on the previous year. Sweden, Denmark and Germany were important importers too. Most of the British coalfields achieved their highest outputs in 1913 when one out of ten workers in this country was employed in the mines. It was the high noon of the industry – although Yorkshire did not reach its production peak until 1924.

In 1914 everything was rosy in the Barnsley coalfield, coal selling at twelve shillings and sixpence a ton,

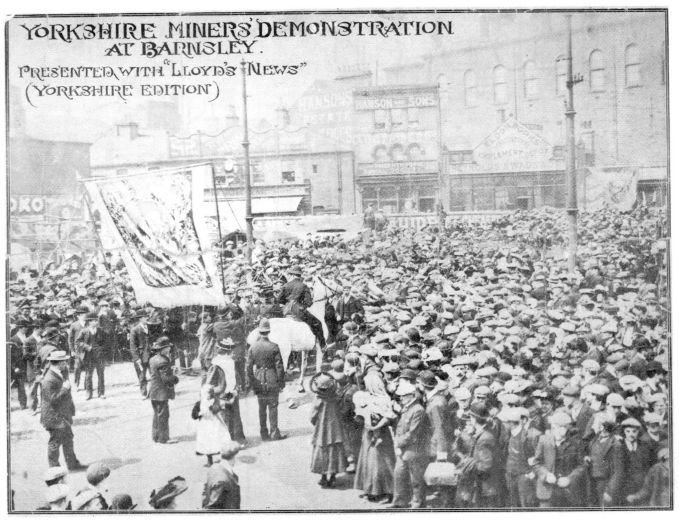

YORKSHIRE MINERS' DEMONSTRATION AT BARNSLEY.
PRESENTED WITH "LLOYD'S NEWS" (YORKSHIRE EDITION)

Right: A miners procession in Eldon Street early twentieth century.
Loaned by G. Beedan, Wombwell.

Below: An unofficial coal mine, Warren Quarry Lane, Barnsley, during the 1912 minimum wage strike.
John Goodchild Collection.

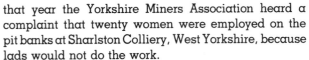

"DON'T GO DOWN THE MINE, DADDY."
1912 STRIKE WARREN QUARRY LANE, BARNSLEY.

compared with nine shillings and sixpence in 1912 and eight shillings and one pence in 1911, and a large steam trawler business had recently announced the signing of a big contract for South Yorkshire coal. With the coal mines booming the owners had problems attracting enough labour to maintain and increase output and that year the Yorkshire Miners Association heard a complaint that twenty women were employed on the pit banks at Sharlston Colliery, West Yorkshire, because lads would not do the work.

The future of the pits, like the future of the British Empire, looked secure but the war changed all that. In August war fever spread across Europe and miners, like other workers, enlisted in the forces in large numbers: it was an adventure and many were glad to see the back of their underground galleries. Between August and April, 1915, 13,000 miners from all the coalfields enlisted, resulting in a shortage of coal which pushed up prices. Although production was concentrated on the home markets, exports to France increased as the war progressed but the lucrative markets in Russia and Germany were lost for ever. In the first year of the war national output dropped by 34 million tons. Absenteeism was said to be a problem, particularly in Yorkshire and court prosecutions against miners who were absent without a valid reason were weekly occurrences. When it was suggested that drink be prohibited, in an attempt to make workers work harder, a Labour MP said absenteeism was due to a number of causes, illness, daily minor accidents and exhaustion.

As the war progressed almost everything in the nation became subject to Government regulations, from the internment of aliens to street lighting and whistling for cabs! Industrial conscription, though talked of, was never introduced to ease the labour shortages. Wage increases and bonuses averted many disputes, although

Above: Hoyland Silkstone Colliery. *J. Grayson, Wombwell*

Above: Ex-miners from the 'Barnsley Pals' (13th Battalion York and Lancaster Regiment) volunteer for newly formed tunnelling companies. They were soon to be engaged in a dangerous game of mining and counter-mining in the Ypres Salient. "Buller", the Battalion mascot sees them off.

Above: Survivors after the Cadeby mine disaster, 1912. *Yorkshire Mining Museum.*

machines for getting the coal out of the ground. By 1917, following the slaughter on the Western Front, the Government switched priorities by announcing to release 500,000 men from the mines for the armed forces. The men to be called up included the following classes: the men who had entered the pits since August, 1915; surface workers and the men who supervised them; and the workers of military age who during the past two or three months had lost on average two or three shifts from an avoidable cause. A coal owner told the *Chronicle*: "It means the men must do their duty in the pits or in the forces. It will put the fear of God into the heart of the young, irresponsible shirker, and the sending of a small proportion to the Colours will remedy the evils of absenteeism. The young devils think more of their pleasures than the needs of the gallant men fighting in the trenches." There were no objections from the Yorkshire miners association, the president of which said difficulties would be created in the forces unless the men were released. But he warned that the men would want their jobs back after the war and he believed the end of the war was in sight.

After the war the mines remained under Government control for a time. With trouble brewing in the coalfields the Sankey Commission recommended a pay increase, shorter working hours and the nationalisation of the mines on a permanent basis. But the Government dragged its feet and by 1921 the post war demand for coal was less acute: the mines were returned to the hated coal owners and the stage was set for the 1926 General Strike.

BATH TUB AND COAL

Back in the 1950s my father talked of the old miners he had known in the 1920s and 1930s. They were born in the 1880s, had received an elementary education and had unusual beliefs: hot water weakened the back and lower limbs and encouraged illness, they said, and they did not like the idea of pithead baths. Their ethos revolved around toughening the body and keeping it in perfect condition to enable them to continue working, since medical treatment cost money. Joe Hall, who started work in 1899 and who later became a national figure, said: "I remember washing at home, with my mother dusting my back. We rarely washed our backs and lower limbs because it was said to weaken them. How my mother kept the beds so clean I will never know."

In Wales they disliked washing their backs because they feared it caused a roof fall. This superstition was not confined to miners: fishermen in Wales did not wash during periods of good catches for fear of washing their luck away. This anti-bathing fear must have taken root in Barnsley in the late nineteenth century because a solicitor reported to a government inspector in the 1830s that Silkstone miners, both male and female, bathed in the same room at the same time with the front door open! Mr Hall, the miners' leader, said it took the union thirty years in the early twentieth century to persuade some branches to accept the idea of pithead baths and one branch

trouble bubbled under the surface and occasionaly broke out in strikes: 170,000 miners were on strike in Yorkshire for a spell in 1914, over the minimum wage, and there was so much disruption in South Wales the coalfield was brought under Government control, a year before the other coalfields.

One problem would not go away – drinking. Drunkenness and absenteeism in industry led the Government into controlling licensing hours through the Central Control Board (Liquor Trade) in 1915. This led to some strange court appearances in Barnsley. Treating a group of friends to a drink became an offence. A group of miners from Wombwell appeared in court in the spring of 1916 after treating each other to drinks at the George Hotel and the landlord was fined ten shillings. At the end of May a Cudworth landlord was fined for allowing "treating" on his premises.

In May, 1916, the coal famine led the Government to talk of suspending the Eight Hours Working Act, reducing the minimum working age from fourteen to thirteen and employing women on the colliery surfaces. A local coal owner said all the pits were under strength, both underground and on the surface. He said the men who had started work after August, 1915, were making up to some degree for the men who had enlisted but they were still inexperienced and there were few

Left and Below: Scenes in miners' homes, 1912.
British Coal, Eastwood Collection.

Above: The days of the old tin bath in front of the coal fire are shown in this photograph by former Wombwell photographer the late Joe Short, whose sister, Mrs Rose Hirst is in the tub and another sister Mrs Emily Glover is in the background.

muscles. I'll aways remember coming home from the war on leave and my mother saying: 'Guess what! Your father has started using the pit baths!' " The back was important. Arms and legs could be strengthened and hardened but the back had a tendency to let the miners down when they least expected trouble. So when they turned their back on superstitions and started washing their backs, they still took care of them, as in the case of my father who wore a cloth belt to support the small of his back. His was a back that seemed to be perpetually smothered in iodine and lotions of all kinds of colours and strength. The accepted wisdom seemed to be that if it did not sting, it did not work. All those bottles of lotions, often bought off the shelves of the corner shop, were supposed to heal cuts and bruises and cure all kinds of aches and pains which afflicted miners. However, despite all the care and attention, the back still caused problems, some miners developing "buttons", scabs on each of the vertebrate caused by rubbing their naked backs against the rock roof.

According to George Orwell the middle classes claimed that miners would not know how to bathe themselves even if there were more pithead baths. After a visit to miners' homes in Wigan in the 1930s, Orwell said a large number of miners were completely black from the waist down for at least six days a week. "It is impossible to wash all over in their homes — every drop of water has to be heated up (on the coal fire) and there is no room for a proper bath in the small rooms." Orwell estimated he would have to take two baths to remove a day's mine grime and 10 minutes to remove the dust from the eye-brows. However, he noted that the myth that washing the legs caused lumbago was dying out. Mine owners were reluctant to provide pithead baths on grounds of costs. Between the wars the owners, convinced that nationalisation was always round the corner, baulked at the idea of investment, not only on the surface but underground.

Coal and dirt were an integral part of a miner's life of course. The hewers hacked away at the coal at work, had a healthy respect for it because they knew that one slip could end in death or injury and they burned it in prodigious quantities at home where it was seen to be as valuable as money in the bank, better than money in a very hard winter. The wages derived from cutting it at work put clothes on their children's backs, paid the bills and provided them with small luxuries.

It had other uses. It was sucked to relieve indigestion, was thought to be a sign of good luck (soldiers have been known to carry a piece into battle; burglars used it as a charm against arrest), was used by craftsmen to make figurines of miners or miniature coal tubs for display in people's homes, was crushed and put on lettuce to ward off slugs and was given to pigs to empty their bowels in preparation for slaughter.

Before radio and television became popular, the fireplace was the central attraction in any home and miners' children spent long winter evenings peering into the coal fires. It was easy to see "pictures" in the blazing coals and dying embers, an amusing and

spent five years trying to persuade their members to hold a ballot on the issue. In 1923, when there were one million mineworkers in the country, there were eleven pithead baths. In the North East in the 1920s it was thought that coal dust toughened the back and miners refused to wash it off. During the 1926 lock-out miners in that area played football with workers in other industries — the miners did not wear shirts and the players and spectators could differentiate between the two teams by looking at their backs, the miners having skin as black as the night. Mr. Jack McKenning, the former chief executive of CISWO who lives in Barnsley, grew up in the 1920s and 1930s and his father rarely washed his back. "He came home from work and bathed all over in the zinc bath in front of the fire — except for his back," said Mr. McKenning. "I then rubbed his back with rough cloth and after a while his back had a polished look about it, like ebony. He believed frequent washing weakened the back

Left: A mining family at Flockton, nr. Wakefield.
Yorkshire Mining Museum

imaginative pastime in the days before soaps and computer games became the predominant occupation of children. The superstitious saw other things in the fire: if the coal burnt unusually bright it was said to be a sign of frost on the ground; a cluster of sparks on the chimney back a sign that news was on its way; a white or black film on the bar denoted a stranger was en route to the home.

Miners loved enormous fires. Thanks to their concessionary coal allowance they were rarely short of coal; whereas other workers would think twice before putting coal on their fires in cold weather, because the fuel was expensive, miners would think nothing of using a bucket full — every twenty minutes if necessary. They derived a sense of pride in the size of the fire. Each home coal delivery was inspected with care, since its quality could vary from month to month and by the late 1960s and early 1970s it was felt by some miners that the coal was deteriorating: the best coal for domestic consumption had been dug and sold in earlier times and the contemporary coal had been produced for a different market, perhaps the power stations. Silkstone seam coal had been regarded as very good domestic coal. It was known in some quarters as Peacocks owing to the beautiful colours it contained. The colours gave evidence of the coal tar in the coal and formed the base of aniline dyes. In the old days there was coal that produced a sluggish and prolonged fire and coal that was said to be gassy, spluttering and firing bits around the hearth in the early stages of ignition and then settling down to a roar that could be heard round the room with even the smallest lump producing a fierce flame and bubbling coal tar. As the fire went into top gear the coals became a crimson mass of heat that made the occupants push their chairs away from the

fireplace or Yorkshire Range in a bid to keep cool. This was the kind of fire a miner loved: it burned swiftly and had a healthy appetite, having to be fed with coal at frequent intervals. It had to be a very hot day before a miner was prepared to peer at an empty grate. It has been suggested that miners needed big fires because they were accustomed to intense heat at work. Writing in the March, 1993, edition of *The Dalesman*, a woman told the writer, Mr W. R. Mitchell: "After the warm conditions underground heat was as important as food. He must have a big fire. I remember one day, a few days after we were married, we returned home from a shopping expedition to Pontefract to find the fire was out. It wasn't vital to us but Dick — who had been reared in a miner's home — had never experienced a cold grate in the living room. He actually cried." There was always something emotional about a coal fire; on a cold and wet evening the sight of flames roaring up the chimney swelled the heart and I have always associated an empty grate with sorrow and loneliness. Lawrence wrote of a collier's home: "All the life of the room seemed to be in the white, warm hearth and the steel fender reflecting the heat." Writing of his childhood home in Fitzwilliam, near Pontefract, Geoff Boycott, the cricketer, stated in his autobiography: "A place of warmth, movement and caring, a little part of a true community which now seems outmoded and old fashioned."

Large buckets and shovels were indispensable in the home. My uncle's next door neighbour, with the tongue firmly in the cheek, often complained that he was awakened at seven a.m by my uncle who, having got the fire going, threw a large bucket of coal on the fire, always ensuring that the coal bounced off the fire-back for effect and as a result made so much noise

Above and Right: The blacksmith's shop at Monk Bretton Pit, 1912.
Don Booker

and vibration both houses in the terrace shuddered. My uncle did not realise he was a nuisance, for all miners threw buckets of coal on to the fire with some force, since to do otherwise would have been a sign of a weak man.

Coal dust was rubbed into wounds and grazes to facilitate healing. Old miners said they had enough coal dust inside them, after a working life down a mine, to keep them warm for the rest of their lives. Their backs were pitted with blue scars caused by coal dust embedded in the skin: according to one local woman her father's back was like a road map of England, with all the blue specks, small holes and blue lines. A layer of coal dust was seen as a badge of courage. Mr Hall, after his first shift underground at Darfield Main Colliery, refused to remove the dust for several hours because he was so proud of his blackened features, a confirmation of his adulthood. That kind of ritual was not confined to future miners' leaders. Fresh from his first day down a mine a young miner in the 1920s or 1930s would wash, dress and then walk down the street proud of the dark circles round his eyes, the circles having been created by coal dust engrained in the skin. Some miners would eat a meal before bathing. "This is not dirt — it's pit muck and it's clean muck," a miner would tell his wife, who had urged him to get washed. An illogical comment perhaps but it does show that miners had a respect for the stuff. Coal dust intrigued Henry Moore, the sculptor. Commenting on his work as an artist down the pit, he said: "First there was the difficulty of seeing forms emerging out of the deep darkness, then the problem of conveying the claustrophobic effect of countless wooden pit props, two or three feet apart, receding into blackness, and expressing the gritty, grubby smears of black coal dust on the miners' bodies and faces." When the dust lodged in the lungs, leading to that dreaded disability, pneumoconiosis, it was a different story: dust was something to hate and fear. Old miners out for a walk can still be seen leaning, say, on a wall half way up a steep hill, immobilised by this lung disorder. The affliction has now almost disappeared among younger miners, thanks to all kinds of safety measures implemented underground in the 1970s.

Few workers could have had such a close relationship with the product of their labour. For obscure reasons miners retained large chunks of coal for decades. One of our neighbours, the late Walt Dobson, High Street, Wombwell, kept a lump of coal he had cut at Houghton Main Colliery in 1922 for sixty years; ten years ago it was used as the focal point at an exhibition on mining at the local parish church. (In May, 1993, the lump was on display at Barnsley Library). Another piece of coal weighing 156lb., mined at Darfield Main Colliery shortly before the 1926 dispute is now at the Cusworth Hall Museum, near Doncaster. The lump was part of a home coal load delivered to a Wombwell man who, because of its enormous size, refused to break it up. He kept it in the coal cellar for fifty years. When he died at the age of seventy-three his family honoured his wishes that it be kept for sentimental reasons and it was taken to his son's home in Essex, where it remained until 1987. Then the family decided that as it had come from the old Barnsley Bed seam it should be presented to a mining museum — hence its final destination. Miners also became attached to smaller pieces of coal. Recently, I have come across the story of a miner who appeared at the Yorkshire miners' gala in Sheffield in 1909 with a fancifully decorated pick shaft, attached to which was a piece of coal he had won in 1856. At that same gala there were lots of men carrying pick shafts, polished to the last rub, and decorated with flowers.

Coal wielded an almost magical fascination to some men. Many miners hated the sight of coal, having blamed it for turning them into underground slaves; others could not keep away from it. Every village, perhaps every street in the old days, had a character who was strong in the body and weak in the head who spent his spare time shovelling loads of home coal into miners' cellars for a few shillings. He would clear three or four tons of coal per morning or afternoon without any effort or grumble. Monetary gain was not always the principal motivation for this work, for one man I knew tried to commit suicide during the 1984/85

strike (during which no coal was delivered except on compassionate grounds) because he thought no one wanted him. The work had helped the shy and awkward man to forge social contact with his neighbours. My uncle, even in his seventies, would put a couple of tons of coal into neighbours' coal sheds or cellars in a day without a complaint; in his case he appeared to need the physical work to satisfy some inner compunction, since he never asked for a penny. Other shovellers would not accept payment but welcomed a couple of buckets of coal, the best bargaining counters in a mining village.

Coal in the shed or cellar was a valuable commodity. One of our neighbours kept coal in the shed for years and I don't think they wanted to burn it. They hoarded it like gold. In the midst of a bitter winter in the early 1950s the children in the yard were fascinated to see that the door had been left open and the shed was empty except for two or three layers of large lumps of coal. It was the first time we had seen that shed almost empty since it had been built. The size of the lumps intrigued our small minds, as the lumps dwarfed the cobbles of coal that had become the norm for home deliveries in the 1940s and 1950s, and we had not seen anything like them before. Within a few days, however, a new delivery of cobbles from the pit had been shovelled into the shed, covering the old coal once again, saving it for another winter. The lumps were in a way the family silver: in the worst scenario they would not be burned in their home but exchanged for money or other goods. Fortunately, for

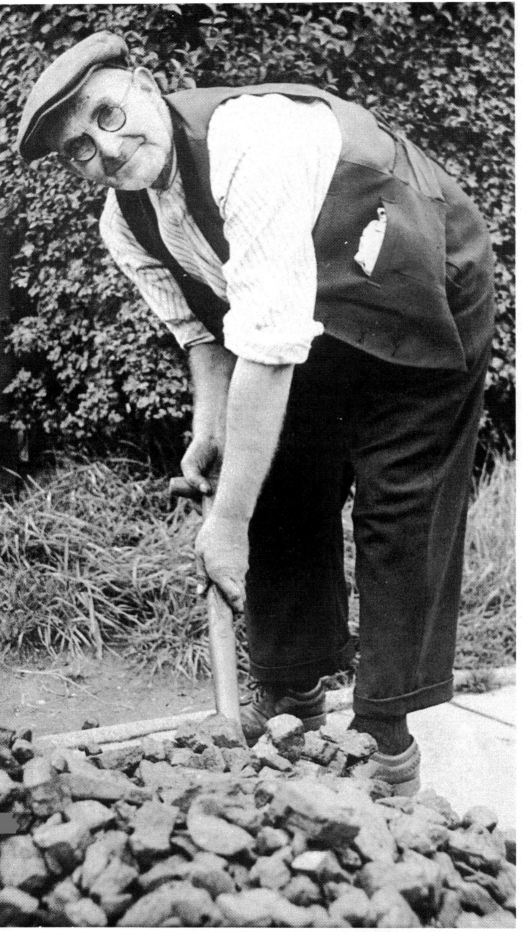

Above: All miners had to start shovelling coal when they arrived home and saw their concessionary coal heaped in the road or the yard. The coal was stored in the coal shed or cellar.

that couple, scarred by their experiences in the 1920s, the bad old dole days did not return.

As the old lady, a born survivor who has street sense, says in the 1941 British film *Love on the Dole*: "I knows nothing about politics but I knows about a load of coal." Which is not as daft as it sounds. In this major film the young idealist dies penniless in bed but the old lady, the queen of street bartering in the terraced streets of Salford in the 1930s, survives on her ten shillings (50p) a week pension and her nose for acquiring buckets of her neighbours' surplus coal which she later burns in her home or sells at a profit.

A DISASTER

By the twentieth century the titantic disasters involving hundreds of victims belonged to the history books but some accidents continued to capture the headlines. Seven men were killed when they were hurled to the bottom of the pit shaft and six others injured, three of them seriously, in the cage disaster at Barrow Colliery on November 15, 1907. Sixteen men got on the double-deck cage when it was lowered to the Parkgate seam. Then it was lowered to the Thorncliffe seam, where the horsekeeper, the only man to travel from the surface, was set down. When the signal was given to ascend the cage gave a tremendous jerk upwards and began to swing violently, throwing six men from the top deck and one from the lower, and they fell sixty to seventy feet to the bottom of the shaft. The other men were thrown off their feet and all the miners' lamps went out. Realising something was wrong the engineman stopped the cage half way up the 480 yard deep shaft; then it was lowered to the Parkgate seam where the men were rescued.

One of the survivors, George Hargreaves, said: "We were thrown off our feet and some could not speak. The others shouted for the cage to stop, for we thought if we came to the descending cage we would be thrown out. It was a fearful thing and seemed to last three quarters of an hour. We dare not move for we did not know what was coming next, and all we could hear was the groaning in the cage." After finding six bodies in a heap in the shaft bottom, the under manager at the Silkstone pit, Mr B. Miller, a member of the rescue team, said: "They were smashed to pieces. One had the head almost knocked off and another an arm almost wrenched out of the socket. It was a horrible sight; it almost makes me sick to think of it." The cause of the accident: the flat iron sheet thrown from the mouth of the shaft to the cage to allow the men to pass from one to another had not been lifted away when the cage had started to ascend. The sheet held the cage for a few seconds and then, releasing itself with a jerk, the cage went swinging up the shaft and the men were thrown out. The jury returned a verdict of accidental death and of gross negligence and carelessness on the part of the two men who were supposed to make sure all was clear before the cage moved.

That same year Mr Frank Chandler was awarded

BARROW COLLIERY.

T COPE C ADAMS T.W.JENNINGS BYAS ROOKE ISAAC FARRER FRANK DOBSON

DISASTER AT BARROW COLLIERY NEAR BARNSLEY 15 NOV 1907

The Barrow Colliery disaster Nov. 1907.

Above: Damaged pit lamps found in the cage;
Left: The remembrance card;
Below: The funeral of some of the victims at Worsbrough Church.

BARROW COLLIERY DISASTER
FUNERAL OF SOME OF THE VICTIMS AT WORSBRO CHURCH

Above: The Edward Medal.

Right: Frank Chandler, of Jump.

Below: Hoyland Silkstone.
John Goodchild Collection.

the Edward Medal for helping to rescue a man in an accident at an underground boiler-house at Hoyland Silkstone Colliery, Platts Common. Chandler's nineteen year old son died in the accident. A group of men were repairing the boiler-house in the Parkgate seam when a large girder collapsed, bringing down with it a section of the roof: the boiler and piping burst and there was an escape of scalding steam. One man died on the spot and three others were so seriously injured they died in Beckett Hospital, Barnsley, three days later. At the inquest Chandler, a deputy who was in charge of the party, said they were working on the brick walls on which the girders rested. "There was a big earth bump, my lamp was knocked out and I was scalded by escaping steam. I found a man called Cooke in an exhausted condition; I got him on my back and crept away to a place of safety." Then Chandler went back to the boiler-house and heard men shouting, including his son Leonard, who said: "Don't come in here, father, you'll get killed." Realising he could not help his son, Chandler crept along in the darkness until he felt the shaft. Tumbling into the cage he was taken to the surface. Later he was told his son had died. After the coroner at the inquest had said Chandler had displayed great courage, he replied: "I do not think I have done more than any other man would have done." The jury returned a verdict that the four men died accidentally, owing to an earth bump causing the girder to break. They added that the manager was to blame, but not criminally, as the girders were not strong enough to withstand the weight of the roof.

Preparing faces for the resumption of work after the holiday, thirty men were working at Wharncliffe Silkstone Colliery at Whitsuntide, 1914. Coal cutting machines were being used in the thin Whinmoor seam when there was an explosion and a sheet of flame and accompanying firedamp swept through the workings, killing eleven and injuring four. A hurricane of stone and dust lifted two deputies off their feet,

HOYLAND SILKSTONE COLLIERY

The Wharncliffe Silkstone disaster, 1914.

Above: The pit at Tankersley.
Loaned by Mrs G.A. Greaves.

Left: The remembrance card.
G. Beedan.

Below: The jury in the pit yard.

some distance from the explosion, and hurled them fifty yards down a roadway.

A *Barnsley Chronicle* reporter said: "The whole affair, indeed, was a matter of a few minutes, and so confined was the area, that men working in other parts of the pit were unaware of the calamity." The 2,000-man colliery was usually free of gas and no fire was started after the explosion, thanks to the ventilation and the damp conditions underground. After the alarm was raised the under manager and chief engineer went underground without safety apparatus, halting for a few minutes to turn the cloud of firedamp into the return airway with brattice cloth. Within twenty minutes they had reached the scene of the explosion, about a mile from the shaft. The reporter wrote: "It was evident from the conditions of the bodies that the blast had passed them quickly by. In each instance the features were capable of easy identification, the burns, principally of the first degree being on the upper parts of the body and head. In only a few cases was the hair singed or the clothing burnt away."

Meanwhile, the Wharncliffe Rescue Brigade, on descending the shaft, found no reason to don their safety helmets in the clearing air. The bodies were conveyed to the joiners' workshop on the surface. After identifying the body of his son in law in the workshop, which was used as a mortuary, Mr William Walker, a miner of High Green, said Mr William Fisher, his son in law, had been reading an account of an accident in which a miner had been killed a week earlier and had told his wife: "Don't be surprised, Nell, if they bring me home like that." Mr Fisher also said that he believed the coal cutting machines were dangerous and the jury at the inquest heard that a spark from a machine may have caused the explosion. The Bishop of Sheffield, on visiting the bereaved families, said: "There were families of three, five and seven children who had lost their fathers in a moment." The head of the rescue team had told him that a man whose body was badly burnt told the rescuers to help his workmates. "That," said the Bishop, "is what I call courage of the first rank and the man deserves the Victoria Cross."

MEN OF IRON

The brutal side of miners may have been on the wane in the early twentieth century but their lives were still based on muscle power. "It is only by having a muscular body that we can earn a living," wrote Hemingfield miner Joseph Knowles in his diary. They were men of iron, like hammered statues of iron under a smooth black coating of coal dust, according to one writer who forgot to mention in his spasm of elegant prose the ugly grey streaks on the miners' backs down which flowed the sweat. A Vicar of Silkstone, the Rev. J. Prince, writing in his book, *History of Silkstone*, published in 1922 and dedicated to miners, said the grimy black of the miners was only skin-deep and they were in the main hard-working men.

It was this unconscious addiction to both hard work

Above: Boys started work at 13 or 14 years underground. They were often puny (see above) but once they became hewers they developed muscular bodies.
Yorkshire Mining Museum.

and physical prowess – plus their relationship with the nightmarish underground environment and their stoicism – that was the very essence of the coal hewers, the men who cut the coal. As John Wilson, the Durham miners' leader said: "Forcing me to hew lifted me out of the category of boys at a very early stage." The hewers, the elite underground workers, the men who were eulogised by some artists and writers (Auden referred to the "lurcher – loving miner as black as night") had a special quality – strength – and in their eyes that elevated them above other men. Underground they were at home, men who knew every crevice and cranny as well as the temperament of the mine and its seams and who were accustomed to working in deep darkness: "The darkest night is mere twilight compared to the darkness down a pit," wrote Jack Lawson, who started work underground at the age of twelve, became an MP and writer. Outside a coalfield, however, they were more uneasy and did not feel at home in what they saw as an alien world. (Even in the 1980s Arthur Scargill moved the headquarters of the NUM out of London to Sheffield, one of the reasons being that he felt the miners' "home" should be in one of the coalfields).

Like all industries, mining had its slackers and Mondays were seen as unofficial days off, "Colliers' Monday," or "Mabon's Day" (named after a miners' leader) as it was known in South Wales. Being superstitious, miners would not go down a mine under certain conditions; for instance, when a man was killed in the pit the whole pit would stop work that day or on the day of the funeral. But apart from those peculiar customs the average hewer was a

conscientious worker, a man who had a sense of pride in his work. Though it was viewed by the outside world as an unskilled job for many years, the hewer needed skills with which to cut the coal in his stall using various pick heads (striking the coal at the right spot would save him time and effort) and he enjoyed exercising his muscles in the daily contest with the wall of coal. The writer George Orwell said hewing took super human effort but the fact that it was often performed in uncomfortable positions, like crouching or on one's side, made the work even more exacting: he said he would not have lasted a week down a mine. Orwell was not a physical man; he admired miners (to demonstrate his rapport with the working classes he slurped his tea out of a saucer in the BBC canteen)

Above and Below:
Hewers, the elite workers.

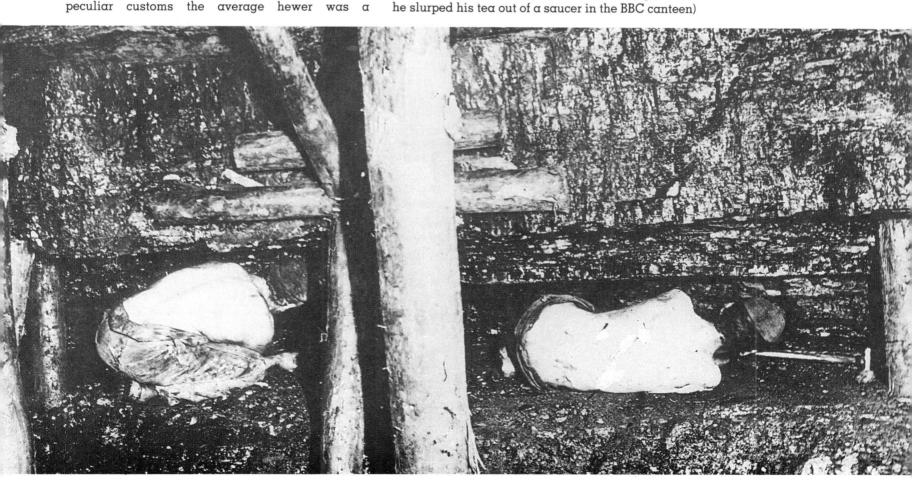

The Wentworth Silkstone Collieries Ltd.

FENTON SEAM PRICE LIST.

		s.	d.
1. Getting, Filling, and Tramming coal, free from dirt, and with lamps, in banks, posts, or headings, including setting and drawing all face timber, per ton		2	9½
2. Heading, End or broken, up to 7 ft wide, per yard		6	0
Heading, Bord, up to 7 ft wide. ,, ,,		5	6
3. Recovering fallen in Banks, ... per yard		3	0
4. Tramming, after first 60 yards, for every 40 yards, or fractional part thereof, ... per ton			¾
5. Pushing up out of low side gates, first 5 yards included in starting price, for every additional 10 yards or fractional part thereof, ... per ton			1½
6. Cutting fast sides, in Banks, where ordered by the Management, for each fast side ... per yard		1	9
7. Setting bars, up to 7 feet long, ... each			9
Setting bars, over 7 ft to 10 ft. long, ... each		1	6
8. Laying square turns, at Gate bottoms, ... each		2	6
9. Laying round turns, at Gate bottoms, ... each		1	6
10. Laying flat sheets, at Gate bottoms, ... each		1	6
11. Colliers, when working for the Company, per day		7	6
Trammers to be paid the same rate, when working for the Company, as the Collier pays them.			
12. Colliers working shift work, per ton			¾
13. Taking side off, for passbyes, etc., up to 3 ft thick, per yard		2	6
14. Building wood packs, filled solid with dirt, each		2	6
Building skeleton wood packs, ... each		1	6

		s.	d.
15. Filling and tramming fallen dirt, ... per tub			4½
Emptying dirt, ... per tub			4½
16. Filling and tramming water, ... per tub			4½
17. Middle packs, 6 ft wide, ... per yard		2	0
18. Ripping or Dinting, in Gates, or Headings, (including tramming the dirt to the passbye, or packing it at the side of the road in Headings, as may be ordered by the management, and putting packs on each side of the Gate in longwall gates) 6 ft wide, per inch, per yard			3
Where the Ripping or Dinting, is less or more than 6 ft wide, the price to be pro rata.			
19. Where faulty and difficult places, or wet places, are met with, and are not provided for in this list, the remuneration shall be agreed upon between the Officials and Workmen.			
20. Drawing rails off disused Gates, per yard of road drawn off			1½

The above are basis prices on the 1911 rates, which includes 50% on the 1888 rates, and are subject to the rise and fall of district percentages.

Signed on behalf of the Wentworth Silkstone Collieries Ltd.

JAMES WHITFIELD.

Signed on behalf of the Workmen.

ALBERT DARLOW,
FRANCIS M. WHITEHEAD.

Signed on behalf of the Yorkshire Miners' Association.

THOS. PHIPPS,
GEO. HY. HIRST.

16th November, 1918.

Above: The price of coal.

but his lack of physical prowess would have been secretly abhorred by miners, who still retained some elements of the old tribal system (see *The Early Miner*). They despised anything that was soft or appeared to be soft. That love of muscle-power and work formed two of the acknowledged but unstated rules of a kind of exclusive miners' club from which even their wives and children were often excluded. In their impromptu groups at work and in their spare time the miners indulged in what they regarded as elitist talk about the cleavage of coal, "wooden" (hard) coal and the "mini" (minimum wage) and about their pastimes: dogs, pigeons and sport. The groups, large and small, were found in many locations. All towns and villages seemed to have a favourite spot where miners gathered, such as a street corner where they stood deep in conversation, hands deep in pockets, watching the world go by. In Barnsley it was at the bottom of Market Hill, in Wombwell outside the Prince of Wales (when there were more than six standing outside the public house, it was seen as a sign that one of the pits was on strike or on short time). Miners also met on allotments, in the tap-room of public houses or back-yards. The discussions, mainly for the edification and enjoyment of the participants, also had the subliminal effect of enhancing the cameraderie among miners.

Down a mine men's safety depended on the men standing next to them, all of which formed a vital bond, and that sense of cameraderie ran through their lives like a vein. It also formed part of the texture of the union, for that bond was essential during any strike; most miners realised that one "black leg," a renegade, could break a strike. Workmen from other industries, particularly if they had less physical jobs, were often secretly despised and were discouraged from taking part in "pit talk." As one ex-miner, Fred Brady, of Thurnscoe, told the *Chronicle* as late as 1993: "When you get four miners together they talk coal because that's the only thing they know."

Coal and work, they were the perennial topics (sometimes it was said more coal was cut in the pub than down the mine). Dick Brown, a miner who worked in South Wales in the 1920s and 1930s said on the television programme, *All Our Working Lives*: "I started work after being indoctrinated by my father and his friends who came to the house. The only topic in the Valleys in those days was work. We accepted that mining was the only way of life. Quite frankly, on reflection, I was scared stiff by the atmosphere of the pit, the conditions, the stench and the darkness. I cried my eyes out and I told my father I did not want to go back, but I had to go to work to live." George Thomas, later Viscount Tolypandy, wrote in his autobiography: "We used to listen to stories about life down the pit as lads and felt quite envious. It sounds incredible today but we listened because mining had a manly image."

Above: A hewer at work in a thin seam in the 1980s. *British Coal.*

Mr John Hunt, a pony lad at South Kirkby Colliery and later a pit manager, said there were three types of workers: those who got on with their work and did not require supervision; those who would work under supervision and those who had to be cajoled or bullied to work. A man would be expected to clear a length of coal measuring between eight and nine yards by about two yards in two days. The quicker he cut it the more money he received; surface workers were paid by the hour. A miner would be expected to buy his tools. Will Paynter, of the South Wales Federation and former general secretary of the NUM, speaking on *All Our Working Lives*, said in his coalfield in the 1920s men had a sharp hatchet (for cutting their own timber for roof supports), several picks with straight blades and a sled to enable the miners to erect wooden supports. Another Welsh miner, Stan Millard, said on the same programme that he had two shovels – "You always had shovels" – a box to put the coal in and a sled as well as a number of other tools he had to buy. A Yorkshire miner wrote in 1929: "Taking my tools into my stall I first of all test for gas to make sure my place is safe to work in. I haven't said much about my mate up to now but very likely he has been with me all the way from the pit bottom. There are four men working in my stall, two in the mornings and two in the afternoons. All our earnings are paid for at piece rates and booked to one number, the whole being shared at so much per shift worked each week. When

I walk down the gate into my stall, I am facing twenty-four yards length of coal face which constitutes the length my mates and I are responsible for working. There are two kinds of work on the coal face – hard and harder."

Miners have always fascinated people from other backgrounds. Artist Josef Herman, in his autobiography *Related Twilights* recalled seeing a group of miners and the image it produced: "This image of miners on the bridge against the glowing sky mystified me for years with its mixture of sadness and grandeur, and it became the source of my work for years to come." Eton-educated and former colonial police officer George Orwell said he felt inferior in the presence of miners. The Vicar of Silkstone, Rev. Prince, born into the middle class, was also intrigued, and writing in *The Daily Mail* in 1919, said he had studied the life of the miner. "It is hard work and only a skilled man can get the coal out. Often he works in water, often in great heat – much depends on the place he gets in the pit. I have known miners who after working all week have not had a living wage left for themselves after paying the hurriers (the men who pushed the tubs). I have tried to understand the miner. It is not difficult: he is a good hearted, industrious fellow, with no wide vision, fond of his beer, his racing, his home; easily influenced, but willing to hear both sides of the question; generally contented." Mr. Prince, who seemed to think miners were akin to children and

Above: A deputy below ground, 1912.
British Coal, Eastwood Collection.

therefore needed parental guidance to help them avoid the pitfalls of life, was involved in an acrimonious debate in the letters column of the newspaper. In 1919 the pits were still under the control of the Government and there were widespread strikes and, of course, miners were blamed in the newspapers for the trouble. While defending the miners, the Vicar blamed the unions for some of the problems, claiming secretaries and officials had a tendency to mislead the men. Then the Vicar criticised the Government, the coal owners (soon to take over the pits again) and the middlemen for profiteering in the past. "When a man deals in coal he soon stinks of brass," wrote the Vicar. "I have seen it again and again over the past ten years — fortunes literally piled up out of nothing. If miners see employers, the middlemen and others riding in a £2,000 Rolls Royce, and stinking of brass, can we wonder why they (miners) want a share of the plunder?" The Vicar appears to have had a sincere regard for miners, though treating them like grown-up children, but like many members of the middle class at that time he found difficulty in coming to terms with the concept of trade union officials and found Communists incomprehensible. He was quick to point out there were no Communists in Silkstone during the 1921 miners' strike... even though his last quote about the Rolls Royce could have come straight off the lips of what was then known as a Bolshie.

The writer DH Lawrence, born in the 1880s, the son of a Nottinghamshire miner, who often wrote about his father's generation, shared the view that to some extent they were innocents with dirty faces, believing miners were quite content with their lot until agitators and sentimentalists stirred them up in the late Victorian period. He believed miners in the 20 th century steeped themselves in work to run away from the home: "Colliers were deeply alive, instinctively. But they had no daytime ambition and no daytime intellect. They avoided, really, the rational aspect of life. They worked together in a kind of intimate community." What Lawrence called "physical awareness" was at its strongest down the mine; when they came up the shaft they "had to change their flow," almost as if the world underground was more relevant to them than that on the surface. "It was hard facts, in the shape of the wife, the money and the nagging home necessities that they fled away from, out of the house into the pit." The writer may have been right up to a point but Lawrence had a tendency to see things that were not there, the product of an overwound or exalted imagination. The miner may have run away from the home, like husbands in all walks of life, but not necessarily to the pit. Anyone who has read of the conditions underground before nationalisation would realise that few men could have worked there for prolonged periods and enjoyed it. The miner romanticised his skills and the pleasure he elicited from work but the three feet high dust-filled seams (the dust was thick enough to throw back the light from a miner's lamp) were something different: no rational person would have run away from home to face the subterranean horrors and the dangers of the coal face where a lump of coal big enough to kill a man could

shoot out of the roof with the speed of bullet and where he worked in fear of the crack of a wooden prop and the ominous dribble of bits of rock or dirt from the roof, often a sign that something terrifying was on its way. Some men feared they were tied to the pit, its slaves, and that horrified them. They saw the walk to the pit as one long queue from which they opted out in an evening only to catch up with again the following morning. To these men pits were seen as transit camps where men worked until something better turned up. Only the unfortunate or the men who enjoyed pit work stayed the course, they declared.

Invariably of medium build, with strong legs, broad shoulders and firm backs, the old fashioned miners had qualities which not only made them eminently suitable for working underground but which made other workers feel uneasy in their company: their physical aura in a room was palpable, almost intimidating to anyone less physical. Again they caused extreme reactions in people. Over-refined women found them repellant, a reaction against their coarseness and omnipotence; other women found them fascinating for the same reasons. Occasionally one of the women who found them fascinating would marry beneath herself, to use an old fashioned phrase, as in the case of Lawrence's mother, a teacher who was intrigued by her husband-to-be, a cavalier who romanticised his working life. But she was soon disappointed. (In the *Sick Collier* Lawrence wrote: "...so intensely himself, like a vigorous animal. And as he shaved, wiping himself, with his naked breast towards her, she felt rather sick, seeing his thick arms bulge their muscles.."). Having faced the reality of mining life — and married life — she regretted the day she had ever met him, her temperament and her taste for refinement (she didn't even like pets which she equated with dirt) being incompatible with life in a mining village. She didn't like miners' interests, their addiction to work or drinking.

These contradictory forces, the human need for culture and education and the other end of the spectrum, miners' work and pastimes, were mirrored in countless homes all over the coalfields, resulting in conflict which had far reaching consequences for some families. A few highly sensitive, intelligent children were lucky. Repelled by what they saw as the barbaric background of the pit village these young people could not wait to leave it all behind, using their stark childhood memories to spur them onto greater things, in literature as in Lawrence's case or in some other form of cultural activity.

The intelligent threw themselves into careers which were the opposite to the working lives pursued by their fathers. The idea that son followed father down the mine is a generalisation. There were many cases of families working at pits for generations but there were an equal number of mining families who were determined not to allow their lads to go underground. Jack McKenning, former chief executive of CISWO who was brought up in the 1920s and 1930s, was told when he was a boy: "If you go near that pit yard, I'll get the belt out..." his father was trying to turn him off pit life while he was still young. Jack went on to work in a

Above: Jump Band, 1912.
F.W. Williamson, Wombwell.

solicitors' office, a travel office and the Yorkshire Miners' Association offices before moving to the Coal Industry Social Welfare Organisation in the 1950s. To many families any job, however menial, was preferable to a pit job. A scholarship to grammar school often resulted in family celebrations, a white collar job was "a bobby's job."

Children who had musical leanings (the Vicar of Silkstone noted in 1922 that miners were fond of music, and many homes had an American organ or piano) but who were unable or disinclined to leave the village channelled their talents into the local brass band or choir. Brass bands such as Grimethorpe achieved remarkable success at national and international level producing music which, like so many things associated with mining, surprised the outside world, its clarity, richness and texture being the very opposite to the dour and dehumanizing life underground and in the village. To outsiders such conditions were supposed to stifle not stimulate artistic talent. The musical miners' preoccupation with their pastime was often a reaction against their working conditions. Whereas the mid-19th century miner had adopted gaudy clothing to cleanse himself of his dirty working environment, some miners in subsequent eras threw themselves into the world of brass bands and choral societies. What is more cleansing than good music? With death or injury just round the corner in their daily lives, the miners needed a release and another world in which to lose themselves. It is also easy to forget the sensitive side of miners. Lawrence always maintained some miners

who looked rough and uncouth had an awareness for beauty that was locked away inside them, a quality that only discharged itself in another of their pastimes, gardening. The writer said he had seen miners peering at their gardens or landscape with an untutored but almost organic eye for nature, describing it as "an indiscriminating feel for nature." Whereas women regarded flowers and plants merely as possessions miners saw them as things of beauty, claimed Lawrence, a mysogynist who believed miners' wives were preoccupied with materialism and paying the bills and therefore had not developed the miners' instinctive eye for beauty and nature.

Miners had another sensitive side, a built-in sonar system, and they could pick up the slightest noise or movement underground. My father was sat in Askew's barber's shop, Wombwell, one day when he sensed a mild earth tremor which went undetected by everyone else in that room. The following day a story in the Daily Express confirmed there had been a tremor, the epicentre of which was some miles away. He also had a remarkable talent for anticipating sudden changes in atmospheric pressure, particularly in the early hours of the morning when he was on his way to work: when the weather changed dramatically and swiftly with a noise like the crack of a rifle shot, he would turn to his mate and say: "Told you so!" When George Thomas, later Viscount Tolypandy, was helping his brother in a makeshift mine during the 1926 dispute, George was suddenly pushed out of the way by his brother and an enormous stone fell out of the roof of the tunnel and landed on the spot where George had

Left: Hoyland Band, 1926.
F.W. Williamson, Wombwell.

Below: Elsecar Pit Band.

been standing. "How did you know that was going to happen?" asked George. "I heard it," came the reply. George, who told the story in his autobiography, "Mr Speaker," said he had heard nothing. His older brother, a seasoned miner, had acute hearing which was essential down a mine where you had to wield a pick or shovel while at the same time listen for the crack of a wooden prop (pre-war miners did not like metal props because they gave no warning) as well as the normal creaks and groans in a mine. It was a long time before miners accepted the idea of wearing helmets despite the obvious advantages, because helmets restricted their hearing. Sound was useful in other ways. Most miners could test the coal or roof by sound; they tapped the coal with the pick and shaft

Right: Harold Larwood, miner turned demon bowler.
Press Association

to see whether it would take a lot of persuading to move and the roof to see whether it was about to collapse. Having to work in such a precarious environment enabled them to acquire a sixth sense: they could "feel the weight on the back" before a roof fall, or so they claimed. It is paradoxical that men renowned for their brawn had a sensitive side to them, sensitive to movement underground as well as to music and nature. Assuming that artists are made and not born, the miners' work created other artistic qualities, amateur writers and painters being not uncommon, and clubs, particularly after the First World War, encouraged such talents and the Ashington group of artists, an evening class of miners in Northumberland in the 1930s became very well known, eventually recording every detail of mining life both on the surface and underground. Books about the Ashington group are still being published in 1993.

But the overriding influence at work and home was the physical side. As well as being indispensable to their survival on the coal face, the miners' physique had other advantages unconnected with work: it opened doors to other worlds. Interest in the mass spectator sports mushroomed towards the end of the nineteenth century and one could write a book, as they say, on the numbers of ex-miners who played league football. It was said that if you needed a centre-forward or 'keeper you just whistled down a mine shaft. Cricket was another sport which attracted miners. Harold Larwood, born in Nottinghamshire in 1904, is regarded as the best fast bowler produced by this country. Having built-up his physique on the coal face no one was better suited to the exacting craft of demon bowling – he had a perfect run up and balance and his wide shoulders and powerful legs enabled him to produce spells of fast bowling which terrified batsmen on the Australian tour in 1932/33. Had Larwood been an office worker one doubts whether he would have had such formidable power in his legs and shoulders, essential qualities in an intimidating bowler. It was not just his physical side; his mental make up had been fashioned down a pit as well and he did not give an inch on the field or give a monkey's uncle about casualties, all of which underlined the cliche that miners worked and played hard. When the Australian captain complained that there were two teams on the field but only one was playing cricket, he was referring to England's bodyline bowling and Larwood, the principal perpetrator, who almost precipitated a riot when he struck the batsman Oldfield on the head with a bouncer. Larwood was bowling leg-theory on the orders of his captain, Jardine, but the fast bowler was seen as the devil incarnate and at one point the public outcry in Australia nearly led to the nation breaking off diplomatic relations with the mother country. Bowling short-pitched deliveries on what appeared to be marble-topped pitches, Larwood gave the batsman a split second in which to decide what to do with the ball – duck or get injured. When Larwood bowled at nearly 100 mph the ball reared and spat off the pitch like a super charged cobra. After the tour Larwood, embarrassed by all the fuss, was put out to grass by

Left: Shaft sinkers at
Elsecar Main Colliery, in the
early years of this century.
G. Beedan.

Left: Primitive pit
somewhere in the Pilley
area.
Mr J. Edwards, Birdwell.

the Test selectors who were afraid he was a threat to
the future of Test cricket. He never played for England
again. Another fast bowler on that tour was a miner,
Bill Voce, who also played for Nottinghamshire. In
Ashes in the Mouth, a book about the infamous tour,
published in 1982, Ronald Mason described him as "a
formidably tall left-hander. Immensely strong, with a
fine high action, he bowled round the wicket with a
tireless aggressive persistence."

Close behind Larwood in the prestigious annals of
fast bowlers was Fred Trueman, the best produced
by this country since the Second World War. The son
of a miner from Maltby Main, Trueman had the perfect
stature for a fast bowler, short and stocky with a wide
beam and powerful legs. The death of mining seems
to have led to a dearth of genuine fast bowlers in this
country. Perhaps a mining childhood would have
improved some other cricketers. Colin Cowdrey had
a middle class upbringing and natural talent but
when he failed to reach his full potential Len Hutton
wrote: "I sometimes wonder how good this wonderful
Kent batsman would have been if he had been brought
up in the back streets of Leeds or Sheffield." Or
Barnsley. Geoff Boycott, the son of a miner from
Fitzwilliam, Nr. Pontefract, may not have had
Cowdrey's grace and style but the Yorkshire man

played as if he believed that failure would put him back down a coal mine, and no one with any sense would want that if he knew the alternative was playing cricket on long summer evenings.

Miners' strength and skills were useful in time of war. During the First World War when stalemate had paralysed the forces on the western front miners were used to try to force a breakthrough. Tunnelling under "No Man's Land" miners placed huge land mines under the the enemy lines; on detonation by the sappers they created enormous craters. The idea was a success at first but the Germans developed counter measures including sensitive listening devices which picked up the sounds of the men tunnelling, and the allies had to wait until the arrival of the American forces, the tank and the exhaustion of the enemy before the final breakthrough came.

No miner could retain his strength for ever and it was time that broke them. That occurs to all men but the decline is accentuated in men who have had a perfect physique in their youth and who end up on the streets as crippled old men. As young men they worked so hard they developed muscles where none had been before and they developed enormous appetites: "Man is a stomach," wrote Jack Lawson. "When fingers, hands, wrists, arms, shoulders, back, body-trunk, thighs, leg balls, feet and toes have been crying aloud, there is only one thing that matters, the stomach." At work they had a meagre diet, a Dudley or bottle of water plus slices of dried or buttered bread and, on special occasions, dripping, contradicting the assumption you cannot work on an empty stomach; at home they had stew meat, vegetables and Yorkshire puddings in prodigious quantities: it all fuelled the great physical machine. And they had big thirsts, although their favourite tipple at work was water which was needed to replenish the sweat. Chewing tobacco also helped to quench a thirst and keep the mouth moist: when he visited a mine in the 1930s George Orwell was horrified when he put his hand in a brown, soggy lump of chewing tobacco which had been discarded on the face. By middle age some miners were physically spent, particularly if they had worked in their teens with their fathers who, of course, would not have been as nimble as in their younger days. Son had to "carry" father on the face, virtually doing two men's work and the work became too much. Miners who did contract work in their youth were susceptible to premature ageing as well. As late as 1970 Sidney Schofield, the Yorkshire miners' general secretary, suggested that miners who had worked in the industry for forty-five years should be given the opportunity to retire. He wrote in his annual report:" There is sufficient evidence to prove beyond a shadow of a doubt that many of our members who went into contract work while they were very young – in their teens or early twenties – are really struggling to work beyond sixty." By 1993 problems regarding miners aged over sixty had almost disappeared. Men in their twenties and thirties were taking redundancy and today a working miner aged over forty is a rare sight.

Below: The great Woolley Colliery, circa 1910.
John Goodchild Collection.

Chapter 3
1920-1940 Strife and Hope

The pits in this country were in deep trouble in the 1920s. Coal demand, production and profits were falling and inflation outstripped wages, all of which set the scene for the 1926 General Strike and the long miners lock-out. Having relied on exports before the First World War to make their profits tick over, the industry now found that nations were producing their own coal or were importing from America and Germany; on the home front the slump dampened the demand for coal.

More than one million miners were employed in the early 1920s (120, 402 in South Yorkshire), each man producing 229 tons per year, compared with 260 in 1913, the peak year in the history of mining. Having failed to use their pre-war profits to modernise the mines, the

Below: Darfield Main branch banner and union members on their way to a gala. Pictured in Low Valley between the wars.

Above: Jump distress committee which fed 1,000 every day. Front centre of the picture is Coun. Preston and his wife.

owners now demanded that the miners work longer hours for smaller wages. The miners, however, claimed their wages had been eroded by a seventy-nine per cent rise in the cost of living since 1914 (in that year miners received six shillings five ½ pence a shift and in 1922 nine shillings four pence). In their annual report for 1925/26, the Yorkshire Mineworkers Association stated: "Coal has been the mainstay of Great Britain. Before the war it was a prospering, fairly tranquil industry and the backbone of the export trade. Now it is a pauper industry, fed by the state, run at a loss and swept by unrest." According to the report, the world shrinkage in the consumption of coal was due to the increasing growth of other sources of power, such as oil and hydro-electricity; the failure to organise and develop the coalfields on more efficient lines; and unsatisfactory international political relations and unrest.

There had been industrial unrest since the end of the war: a strike in Yorkshire over wages and shorter hours in 1919; a national strike in 1920 and a lock-out in 1921 following Lloyd George's decision to hand back the mines – "nationalised" during the war – to the owners. That decision shattered the dreams of miners who had been calling for public ownership since the late 1880s. There had been a glimmer of hope in 1923 when a Bill to nationlise the mines was submitted to parliament, prompting Mr Sam Roebuck, the Yorkshire miners' general secretary, to comment: "Nationalisation is now just a matter of politics." However, the miners had to wait until 1947 before their dream came true.

The General Strike was inevitable. For years there had been a feeling that one day the growing power of the trade unions would result in a large-scale clash with big business, behind which stood the all-powerful state. In the early 1920s government kept quiet and prepared to smash the unions in the event of a General Strike by preparing emergency measures. The short-lived Labour Government of 1924 were aware of the plans but they did not tell their trade union friends, for the government is the government irrespective of political colours and the state is incapable of tolerating threats to its stability and power. The trouble started in 1925 when the Chancellor of the Exchequer, Mr Winston Churchill, put the country back on the Gold Standard, thereby increasing the cost of exports by ten per cent. The pits could not compete with the coal industries in other countries and coal stockpiled at the pitheads. When the owners announced wage cuts and a longer working week, Mr A. J. Cook, the Miners Federation secretary, retorted: "Not a penny off the pay, not a minute on the day." Following a threat by certain unions to support the miners in the event of a strike – it was acknowledged in trade union circles that the miners were much abused – the Government backed away from a confrontation, set up a Royal Commission to suggest proposals to reorganise the coal industry and provided a subsidy to maintain wages at existing levels. Throwing a few crumbs to the miners the Commission recommended that the mines be nationalised at sometime in the distant future; then they said limited pay cuts were inevitable.

The subsidy ran out on April 30, 1926 and the miners, who refused to accept pay cuts and longer hours, were locked-out by the owners. The TUC ordered a General Strike which lasted from May 3 to May 12. With the government maintaining essential services — the plans for which had been prepared over the previous few years — the unions got cold feet and the strike collapsed. Although militant trade union leaders had always maintained that a General Strike would be the first step towards the overthrow of government, most leaders were not extremists and they were frightened that the strike would lead to instability and revolution. The Russian revolution in 1917 and the virulent "Red scares" in America in the early 1920s were still fresh in their minds. Despite the reaction of the other trade unions the miners continued their struggle.

Distress in the coalfields was widespread and union funds soon dried up. On September 2, on the 125th day of the lock-out, a miners' national conference heard that the last money they had paid out was three shillings per head and they had in hand one shilling eight pence per head.

The miners were never solid. Pits in Nottinghamshire continued working and a breakaway union was set up there by an MP called Spencer (history repeated itself in the 1984/85 strike). Miners drifted back elsewhere and the conference in September heard that 400 of the 150,000 Yorkshire miners were working. The miners were locked out for six months and returned to work on the owners' terms.

The lock-out influenced miners' leaders for nearly fifty years. Men like Joe Hall, the Yorkshire president between 1938 and 1952,, lived with the nightmare that

it might happen again, the defeat having rocked the very foundations of the union. Before the General Strike the miners' leaders had been confident of victory: there had been talk of a new world, workers' control of the mines and the end of capitalism. When the union funds started to run out the leaders had to face reality and the humiliation of defeat remained with them for the rest of their lives. That lock-out left its mark on miners' sons who were children in 1926 and who later became miners' leaders. Men like Sidney Schofield, the Yorkshire miners secretary in the early 1970s, came to power fearing that history would repeat itself, that miners would slide into a strike when defeat was inevitable. The impact of that lock-out on the union and miners can never be

Above: A miners' band organised to raise money for strike funds, 1926, in Mapplewell.

Below: A game of miners' golf, nipsy, in the Wombwell and Darfield area.
R. J. Short/Cusworth Museum

Right: Miners' wives soccer team, 1926.
Mrs M. Johnson, Worsbrough Dale.

Below: Making the best of a hot summer nearly 70 years ago at the old brickworks at Darfield Main Colliery.
R.J. Short/ Cusworth Museum, Doncaster.

Above: Swimming in Low Valley, Wombwell, 1926.
R.J. Short

overstated. When Arthur Scargill came to power he was aware of the humiliation and privations suffered by miners, having heard the stories from his father, Harold, a Communist, but he was too young to have been scarred by them and when his generation took on the Government in the 1970s he had none of the hang-ups of the earlier leaders. To him, the 1972 and 1974 victories were sweet revenge.

After the 1926 lock-out things went from bad to worse. Some miners who had been militants during the dispute never worked again, for their names found their way on to the owners' black list. Men who had worked found they were "lepers" in their pit communities and one or two men were still ostracised by people when the 1984 strike started. Demand for coal, and wages, remained low and unemployment rose in the 1920s and 1930s. However, South Yorkshire pits began to produce a greater share of the nation's coal, thirteen per cent in 1929 and 14.7 per cent in 1941. More coal was cut by machine, 13 per cent in South Yorkshire in 1929, thirty-six per cent in 1934 and fifty-six per cent in 1938. By 1935 Doncaster had replaced Barnsley as the coal capital of South Yorkshire.

In the 1930s Mr Joseph Jones, president of the Miners Federation, wrote in his book, "The Coal Scuttle": "The low wages of the miners, their hard uncongenial work and the risk of injury or death, to which they are daily exposed, are all matters which are well-known to their countrymen. There has been a quickening of sympathy for the miners, and there has been a keen desire to come generously to their aid in times of suffering and

distress." Mr Jones, a Mayor of Barnsley, said three main evils dominated the mining areas: unemployment, low wages and oppressive working conditions, adding:" Most people are aware that we have a great unemployment problem; the sad sight of ex-miners begging in the gutters of the cities must bring the fact

Below: Fish being distributed during the 1926 strike: Wombwell or Darfield.
R.J. Short, Courtesy of Doncaster Council, Cusworth Hall.

71

home to the most casual observer." In South Yorkshire the number of miners decreased from 116, 874 in 1929 to 95,947 in 1934; 56,000 were out of work in the whole Yorkshire coalfield the following year. The average wage per year was £114. Mr Jones again: "The knowledge that men who have to face the perils of the pit and who provide the country with the basis of her material prosperity, receive an average of about £2 per week must cause pain and anxiety to all who have pride in their country."

The national production figures rose in the early 1930s from 253 tons per man in 1931 to 280 tons in 1934. During the Depression many pits were on short-time and closed down on two or three days per week and Mr Jones wrote: "The effect of short time working is not disclosed by these figures (the national production figures in the 30s), and this was substantially greater in the post war years than in 1914. If the low wages which have been paid in recent years have not had the effect of reducing the miners' output, it is clear that the output has been maintained at the expense of the miners' families, for unless a sacrifice has been made somewhere, our men could not possibly have maintained the strength and energy which are necessary to carry on the work."

Mr Jones was right when he said there had been a quickening of sympathy for miners during the 30s. There were still some reactionaries in the middle classes, people who believed miners kept coal in the bath, who believed miners were all drunkards and gluttons, but a new generation of writers and film directors were determined to break with the past and they concentrated their talents on the coalfields. George Orwell, author of "1984" and "Animal Farm," was educated at Eton: he did not see a smoking factory chimney until he was adult and yet he identified with the working man, particulalrly coal miners. Gathering material for his

book, "The Road to Wigan Pier," he visited Barnsley, described the hard poverty of families living in Peel Street and Wortley Street and in Mapplewell and toured the underground workings at Grimethorpe Colliery, where he said he felt inferior in the prescence of miners. A.J. Cronin, a popular novelist, highlighted the plight of miners in "The Citadel" and "The Stars Look Down," both of which became popular films. "The Stars Look Down," made in 1939 and starring Michael Redgrave and Margaret Lockwood, is acknowledged to be the first truly British film. Film critics who watched British films in the 1930s not only condemned their inferior quality to Hollywood products but their bias towards the middle classes: many seemed to be set in drawing rooms south of Watford. The few films set in the north portrayed a working class which bore little resemblance to reality and were usually farces or musicals starring Gracie Fields or George Formby. "The Stars Look Down" took a serious look at a mining community and made a plea for the nationalisation of the mines, strong stuff for the commercial cinema at that time. Our feature films may have not been out of the top drawer but we led the way in documentaries, one of the first of which was "Coal Face" which took the film camera underground and showed miners on the coal face. This growing sympathy for miners was in some respects a reaction against their treatment in the 1920s when the nation turned its back on them and allowed the miners to struggle through the lock-out.

It became evident in the 1930s that the measures introduced by the coal owners after 1926, longer working hours and cuts in wages had not changed an industry which was still grossly inefficient. The average man in the 1930s had a social conscience and there was sympathy for the unemployed and the deprived, and for the first time for decades miners had public opinion behind them: they were no longer the national

Below: Grimethorpe Colliery

bogeymen, and the mood of the nation was moving towards the establishment of a fairer society, culminating in the introduction of the welfare state and the nationalisation of the mines after the war. Not until 1992 would miners have so much sympathy again. The closure of thirty-one coal mines in October of that year led to massive demonstrations and a groundswell of opinion against the Government.

1926 = THE LEADERS

Dour Herbert Smith, one of three fascinating men who dominated The General Strike and miners' lock out, was no respecter of persons. Prime Ministers, cabinet ministers and coal owners – and even his own miners, whom he saw as being morally and physically superior to the aforementioned – were handled in a distinctive and irreverent manner by "the man in the cap."

"Nowt doin' ", growled Herbert when things were not going his way. Talks between colliery owners and the union halted and everyone went home ... "Ahr 'Erb" had spoken. He was the dogged, unyielding big boss man of the Yorkshire miners and the Miners Federation of Great Britain during the hungry 1920s. An inverted snob, he sported a flat cap the size of a large dustbin lid and wore an English lever watch the size of small dustbin lid. That was his battle dress: a blatant sartorial warning to his opponents that he relished his working class origins and couldn't be bought. Herbert did not have any finesse, was uncouth, taciturn... but was nobody's fool. Having hauled himself up from the coal face and having met all kinds of men he was a good judge of character. He was also unorthodox, audacious and courageous. And his favourite phrase was "nowt doin'."

Herbert was a big man who attracted tall stories. In 1926 at a meeting in the House of Commons, Lord Birkenhead, who once said that he had never met anyone as stupid as a miners' leader until he met a coal owner, was in evening dress. So was the Prime Minister, Stanley Baldwin, who made an eloquent but long winded speech in which he said the miners had to accept longer hours and cuts in wages. The onlookers gave him a warm round of applause and one or two said: "Jolly good effort, Mr. Baldwin." Preparing to make his reply, Herbert paused and appeared to fumble with his dentures, causing sniggers among the Government supporters, who thought Herbert symbolised everything that was uncouth among miners, who were still regarded as second class citizens. So Herbert paused again and, with the flourish of a Victorian thespian, removed his dentures, wiped them and put them back in his mouth: "Nowt doin'," growled Herbert and sat down. A sea of blank faces stared back at the portly figure from the Yorkshire coalfield. First round to Herbert.

"Fine words do not butter parsnips," was his motto. Born in 1862 he received no formal education ("Books do not produce coal," he said), but he rose through the ranks of the Yorkshire miners, becoming vice president in January, 1904, president in 1906, a post

Above: Children playing in the street, 1920s at Low Valley or Darfield.
R.J. Short

he held until his death in 1938, and president of the federation in 1922, a post he held until 1929. Herbert and his wife, "Ahr Sally" came to Barnsley in 1916, and he became a magistrate, alderman and mayor.

Herbert was a national figure during the General Strike and miners' lock out of 1926. When the other trade unions were reluctant to call the strike, Herbert did not hesitate: "Git onta field," he boomed. When they hesitated again he boomed: "Git onta field," for Herbert did not believe in saying the same thing twice using different words – that's why everyone knew what he meant. Herbert had come up the hard way, earning his sharp trade union spurs in the Woodbine-filled and spittoon-filled union rooms where the art of diplomacy was for nancies and a filibuster was thought to be akin to filling in a man's face: in other words a blow to the face. As Jack Lawson, the MP and author of Smith's biography said: "You could find Herbert Smiths in every mining village, hands in pockets or stood at the street end. He couldn't hide anything and he did not attempt it." Apart from

A.J. Cook, the federation secretary, the other major figure in the General Strike was Baldwin, the Prime Minister, and Smith often clashed with him. The late George Wilkinson, a former NUM official at Houghton Main Colliery, who portrayed Smith in the television series, *Days of Hope*, thought Herbert was the one man Baldwin feared. The men were not unlike each other, although their backgrounds were different.

Baldwin was from a wealthy background and well educated: easy going, almost lazy, and one of his election slogans – "Safety first" – summed up the man. The public saw him as a sound man who did not go in for new fangled ideas; a genial duffer who acted as a buffer against unsavoury ideas that might erupt from the streets or, God forbid, the mine shafts. On the other hand, he had a sincere desire to halt the economic slide in his country and unknown to the public contributed part of his personal fortune towards paying off the national debt. Like many politicians of his generation he looked to the pre-1914 days as the halcyon period and endeavoured to turn the clock back. Smith, born in the 1860s, did not understand the modern world either and had spent most of his life witnessing the expansion of the miners' union (including the 1893 and 1912 victories), not its demise, and a world in which the miners had no political clout was too bewildering for him to contemplate.

Smith wanted to safeguard his members' interests; Baldwin put the nation first, two incompatible ideals. At one point agreement between the Government and the TUC was almost reached in 1926 but unofficial action by printers at "The Daily Mail" provoked the hard-liners in the cabinet and when a representative of the unions went to 10 Downing Street to clarify a point they found the Prime Minister had gone to bed and members of the cabinet had dispersed; the nation tumbled into the General Strike. Earlier protracted talks at 10 Downing Street had their humorous side, however. When Smith strutted into Number 10, the attendant is said to have asked him: "Can I hang up your cap, Mr Smith?" "No thanks," said Smith, "I have lost caps like that before." This is probably an apocryphal story, for photographs from that period show that he wore a flat cap when dealing with his men – to underline his origins – but a homberg when talking to his so-called superiors; but the story illustrates what the man was like. When the miners' council meeting was held the day after the surrender in 1926 a delegate realised Herbert was deflated and asked: "Is our chairman suffering from anthrophobia?" "What's tha' mean?" came the reply. "I think it means fear of your fellow man." "Fear of my fellow man I'll anthrophobia the lot of you before the day is out."

In the lock out Smith was the bulldog; his colleague, Cook, the eloquent dreamer. Whereas Smith was seen as brusque and uncouth – but still a miner – the miners put Cook on a pedestal. One of the most selfless men to hold union office, Cook was the 1920's version of Arthur Scargill, in the sense that he could manipulate an audience of miners as well as fire verbal buckshot at the enemy's rear. It was said he could mesmerise an audience of 80,000 miners. Had you asked the late Jack Woffenden, the hard-headed delegate at Dodworth Colliery in the 1960s and 1970s to name his favourite miners' leaders he would reply: "Cook and Joe Hall – they were great men." Miners always selected the silver tongued as the pick of the bunch. Cook could spellbound miners with his pulpit-style oratory, a reminder that he had been offered at the age of seventeen a place at a Baptist

College. He was born in Somerset but moved to South Wales to work in the mines and that became his power base. Shortly after starting work as a teenager Cook was devastated when a man in the next stall to him was killed in a roof fall. That accident, together with changes taking place in his coalfield, such as falling living standards and the rising power of the newly enlarged coal companies, left a deep mark on him. That underground accident in particular seemed to spur him on to greater things and he always put his members before himself, as if he felt the need to repay some kind of debt; perhaps it was a sense of unjustified guilt arising from that underground accident, perhaps in some small way he felt responsible for it. (It was not unknown for men change places while working). On his way up the union ladder he adopted radical ideals, including the belief that a General Strike could be the first step towards a new world in which the workers would take over control of government. What he forgot was that most miners were more concerned about a living wage than building a new Jerusalem and the establishment regarded him as an enemy of the state, not as a messiah, and newspaper cartoons of that period depict him as an outlaw trying to hold the Government to ransom. The cartoons reflected the opinion of the general public. Cook appealed to the dreamer in miners, the more pragmatic saw him as a dangerous leader. He exhausted himself during the lock-out, having travelled round the country addressing mass meetings of miners, often going without sleep, all of which had a pernicious impact on his health. Although the miners loved him — even in defeat — there were people on their side who saw him in a different light. The intellectual, Beatrice Webb, of the Fabian Society, described him as "an inspired idiot" who was "drunk with his own words, dominated by his own slogans." Miners' leaders said he was capable of inspiring men, like an evangelist, but he was no negotiator. Like Joe Hall, the Wombwell-born Yorkshire miners' leader, he articulated the feelings of inarticulate men, he gave men who had nothing the will to live, to fight for a better future. Unfortunately the General Strike and the lock-out proved too complex and too gargantuan for mere men to handle and the only winners were the cabinet and the establishment, the most powerful institutions in the nation. Cook could not deliver the goods — and I doubt whether anyone else could — and he died a broken man.

One man never forgot Cook. Arthur Scargill is too young to have known Cook but he would have heard stories about the legendary miners' leader from his father, the late Harold Scargill, who lived through the lock-out. On his desk at his Yorkshire miners' offices Arthur had a portrait of Cook to remind him of the bad old days when miners were ground into the dust. Arthur's oratory, his spellbinding speeches much loved by audiences at Yorkshire miners' galas are reminiscent of Cook's. Like Cook, Arthur became the establishment's bogeyman, a man who, they believed, threatened to destabilise society, and the tabloids' editorials of the 1920s were reprinted in a bolder type in the 1980s (when the pound went through the

Right: A week's wage at Cortonwood in 1936.

	Tons	Cwt.	Rate	£	s.	d.
Hand got	18	3	6	1	2	8½
Machine got						
Yardage					6	0½
Sundries					1	9½
2 per cent						
6.1 per cent						
Total				1	11	4½

DEDUCTIONS —	£	s.	d.
Check		1	4
Coals			
Lamps			
Rent		1	7
Insurance			
Death Fund			
Sundries			
Guardians			
Explosives			
Lamp Glasses		2	11
Pick Shafts			
Fines			
JAN 1935	£ 1	8	5½

CORTONWOOD COLLIERIES COMPANY, LIMITED.

No. 834

Payment in Settlement of Wages to date 12 MAY 1936

	Rate	£	s.	d.
DAYS 4	7 -		1	8
4 Special Advance	1 -			4
Percentage 32%				
TOTAL		2	1	9

Stoppages:	£	s.	d.
Home Coals			
Hospital			
Carting			3
House Rent			
Health and Pensions Insurance			
Unemployment Insurance			10
Gratuity			19
Doctor			6
Relief			
Soap and Towels		1	
Baths		1	2
Welfare Fund			2
	1	5	2
Amount due £	1	15	10

exchange floor during the 1984/85 strike the *Sun* had the ridiculous banner headline: "Blame it on Arthur.") But it must not be forgotten that Arthur also modelled himself, unconsciously, on some aspects of Smith's character — for instance, Smith's stubbornness and his refusal to compromise, traits that Cook did not possess, and some people would say traits that prolonged the miners' year long strike in 1984/85.

PONIES

Pit ponies could expect a working life in the darkness and dust: many did not see daylight until they were pensioned off or until the miners went on strike, and a group of pit ponies in a field could be the first sign to the public that there was an industrial dispute underground. The animals were intelligent, often sensing danger before a miner heard or felt ground movement: they were also perceptive, affectionate and sometimes downright bloody-minded, as militant as any miner with a cussedness all of their own.

A large pit like Grimethorpe would have up to 150 ponies, all employed on hauling pit tubs from the coal face to the shaft. The pony drivers were lads, often new to the pit, who built up close working relationships with the ponies, treating them to their "snap" and sweets. Ernest Kay (seventy), Burton Road, Monk Bretton, who spent his early working years at Rockingham Colliery, Hoyland Common, and later at Wharncliffe Silkstone, Tankersley, said on a good day one of his ponies could move forty tons. Joseph Ibbotson (seventy-four), Rotherham Road, Monk Bretton, was employed at Elsecar Main Colliery and recalls his ponies' foibles with affection. Tiger could remove the cork from a water bottle and down the contents in one gulp; even today he wonders how the animal managed it. The pony also liked his snap and would shake the snap tin until the lid came off and the sandwiches fell out. The tin had Tiger's teeth marks on it for years. Wallace had a penchant for clean water and would drink from the trough at the beginning and end of the shift but not from Mr Ibbotson's buckled old bucket at snap time. The bucket was lined with shotfirer's clay and was not the cleanest bucket in the world. "I have seen men drink from that bucket but not the pony. Wallace always spent a long time drinking from the trough at the end of the shift and I was always in danger of finishing twenty minutes late." Tiny, the old pony with bow legs, unhooked the tubs by lashing out with his back legs and then ran off. Another pony had a tail chain twice as long as any other pony's to prevent the driver from being kicked: earlier some men had been carried out of the pit when the pony was in a bad mood. But Toby was the most militant and he had to be banished from the pit because no one would work with him. One man who had worked with horses during the First World War thought he knew how to make the pony move. He put a piece of coal on the pony's bottom and then smashed it with a stick: but the animal did not move.

Many ponies had this stubborn streak. One tub above the allotted number and they would not move until the offending tub was removed. Mr Albert Hayes (seventy-eight), of Grimethorpe, had one or two tricks up his sleeve. When his pony refused to move he rattled the hook on the last tub to con the pony into believing the tub had been removed, and then the pony moved on. "I took carrots along for my pony," he said. "Some of the ponies could look after themselves and needed little supervision. But a young pony, not broken in, could drag the tubs off the rails.

Above: Pit lads and pony.
British Coal, Eastwood Collection.

I can remember my mate coming to the house with the words: "Come on, Albert, let's get down to the pit and get the best ponies." The best ponies were the ones which did not take any coaxing or bullying. At the top of an incline they would halt without instructions and wait for the lad to put the lockers in the wheels to slow down the tubs.

During the 1921 miners' strike the ponies at Grimethorpe Colliery were brought to the surface and races organised, the riders being supplied with jockey caps and whips. Ponies, like miners, had their fair share of injuries and fatal accidents and miners resented the recriminations when a pony was killed.

"There was always an inquiry; management seemed to think more of the ponies than the men. We were told ponies were expensive to buy and keep," said a retired miner. But they did not have an easy life. Lads enjoyed impersonating cowboys a few hundred feet below ground. The practice was supposed to be banned but that did stop Wild West scenes in the roadways; so management employed a man with a bucket of whitewash to splash the riders as they cantered past in the dark, and the culprits with their tell-tale splashes on their clothes were sent to see the manager.

Many miners had more faith in their ponies than in

77

Above and Right: Pit ponies, courtesy of *British Coal Archives.*

78

some of their mates. Mr Ibbotson found himself alone underground one day, the pit deputy having forgotten to remain behind to make sure everyone had finished the shift. When his lamp went out he found himself in darkness as black as a Bible. His pony led him back to the shaft, the miner stumbling over the bags of stone dust in the roadways, the nimble-footed pony missing the lot. Mr Thomas Beedan, whose grandson, George, still lives in Wombwell, refused to leave his pony, Jasper, behind when fire engulfed Cortonwood Colliery in 1904. "There is no room for the pony in the cage," said the manager. "Then you had better find room," came the reply and Jasper was put in the cage and taken to safety. George Beedan said one of his friends, John Wraith Cusworth, of Hemingfield, was once asked why he took hot tea and cold water down the mine. "The tea is for the pony and the water is for my lunch," he replied.

When you talk to old miners about the early days, the one common thread of conversation is pit ponies. It's the only time some of them smile because that was their happiest period down the mine. Eventually they would be found other work — on the coal face perhaps — and other lads would take over their ponies. The job of the hewer was onerous, and the conditions in which the work was performed were often appalling: few men have happy memories of that

Above: Frank Barratt with his pit pony, Dodworth Colliery, 1921.

NOTICE.—The reader is asked to imagine that an " old " and " worn-out " Pit Pony is telling the story of its life " underground."

The Life and Adventures of a Pit Pony

" Life stories," of " Famous Men," are published far and wide
And life stories of " Heroes," who for their country died
My life story may interest you, as ever since my birth
My life's been spent, deep down below, in the " bowels " of the earth

For years and years I've worked and done, my duty faithfully
And tried my very best to serve, the Colliery Company
But now my " working " days are " done," I'm " old " and " worn-out " too
So my adventures down the pit, I'll just relate to you

My home's as near " pit bottom " as, it's possible to be
And when my " shift " is ended, that's the place I long to see
But many times when I've reached home, and my " task's " been none too light
They've fetched me out again before, I've hardly had a " bite "

I've had all sorts of " drivers," some were very, very kind
I've also had some drivers, the worst " brutes " you could find
For instance No. 1 I had, he'd treat me like a " Hog "
And if a tub got " off-the-road," he'd kick me with his " clog "

His orders were, my run of tubs, was limited to " four "
But when there was no one about, he'd " hang-on " many more
Sometimes he'd put on " twenty-tubs," which made my legs fair " totter "
And if I could not " pull," them, he'd " bash " me with a " locker "

Driver No. 2 I had he was a pal to me
He'd often bring a " carrot " or, a " turnip " for my " tea "
A knob of sugar, now and then, when my " shift " was " completed "
And best of all he'd always see, that I was NOT " ILL-TREATED "

He used to drive a mate of mine, old " Tony " was his name
And " Tony " often told me that, he served him just the same
And when my mates at " week-ends," had " extra " work to do
They hoped the lad to fetch them out, was driver No. 2

One day with colliers on the " face," for " water " he was " tapping "
It flooded out the " stalls " while I, was in the passbye " snapping "
He " waded " thro' waist deep to me, " released," and sent me " home "
And then was " carried " back again, by the awful " raging-foam "

Alas, poor driver No. 2, he's in " ETERNITY "
And what is more I feel quite sure, he gave his " life " for me
And when he gets to " Heaven's-Gates," if the good old " Bible's " true
The " King-of-Kings " will say to him, " PASS " Driver No. 2

Driver No. 3 I had, was very hard to please
He'd never try, to see that I, was working at my " ease "
And when thro' " roofing " down a " gate " my " back " was rubbed " red-raw "
He'd merely put some " tub-grease " and, some " coal dust " on the " sore "

Driver No. 4, I had, he was a " football " lad
'Twas, " football " this, and " football " that, aye, he was " football " mad
He'd backed 3 " homes " and 3 " aways," won the " sweepstake " I'll be bound
And nearly got his " coupon " right, to win £1,000

Each " run " on to " main level," he didn't half used to " chin "
And with the other " drivers " he'd, be filling " Coupons " in
He'd then discuss the " Sweepstake " held, at several of the Clubs
And then he'd tell the colliers that, he'd had to wait for tubs

I had a pal named " Jerry " once, who used to " run " a " drift "
He lost his life thro' " carelessness," whilst working out his " shift "
And when he passed me in a tub, he looked an " awful " wreck
The " door-trapper " had fell asleep, and Jerry broke his neck

I have some " happy " memories, as well as sad ones too
The " happiest " is that " 13-weeks," From April " 22 "
The " Pit-Ponies St. Leger," the " field " beside the " dyke "
I told you all about it in my " Memory-of-the-Strike "

There's one thing that I really think, the " public " ought to know
That's how they treat us ponies, who work deep down below
Our " miners " work, one shift per day, and what I fail to see
Is why we sometimes work 2 shifts, and very often 3

They say that for the " coal " we draw there's " royalties " for the " knobs "
The " royalties " we usually get, are " sticks " and " whips " and " clogs "
No doubt they feel quite flattered as, they at their " Mansions " gaze
But scores of times I've never seen, my " home " for several days

We're only poor " dumb " animals, don't think I've got a cheek
We cannot say when " tired " or " ill ", because we cannot speak
But all you drivers down the pit, a word I'll say to you
Be kind and treat your pony as, my driver No. 2.

There's one thing I should like to see, I'll tell you if I may
And that's a " WEEKLY " visit from, the R.S.P.C.A.
A daily " record " of our work, for inspectors, to survey
Also to see we are not worked, above 8 hours per day

Another thing concerning us, that I would recommend
Is that we're brought up in our turns, to " Daylight " each week-end
And now dear reader will you help, to let the country know
There's " still " room for " improvement " in, our " treatment " down below

All the "drivers" in this poem are "fictitious" and do not refer to any living person or persons.
      A.M.

Right: Pit pony races at Darfield.
R.J. Short/Cusworth Museum.

DARFIELD
Pit Pony Races
For the benefit of the Distress Fund.
Thursday, June 16th, 1921
In the big Field between Darfield and Ardsley.

FIRST RACE AT 5 P.M.

PROGRAMME.

Patrons:
C. H. TAYLOR, Esq., J. E. MITCHELL, Esq.,
J. BRASS, Esq., R. WATKINS, Esq., H. HESKETH, Esq
W. DALLAS, Esq., E. TAYLOR, Esq., G. H. HIRST, M.P.

Judge: A. L. GWRAM, ESQ.

Starter: MR. NORTON HARRISON.

Clerks of the Course:
Messrs. J. WORRELL, T. LLEWELLYN, W. WATTS,
and G. RITCH.

Stewards:
Messrs. A. JOBLING, HODGSON, SWAIN, and AVILL

Houghton Main Colliery Prize Band and Wombwell S. & S.
Comic Band will play selections in the Field and also parade
the principal Streets.

PROGRAMMES 1d. EACH.

All the Prizes have been given by local gentlemen.

T. M. Thornaby & Son, Printers, Wombwell.

work. But for all the amusing stories about ponies, and for all the palpable affection between the ponies and the lads, there were cases of brutality which led to the 1911 Mines Act permitting the owners to appoint inspectors to look after the interests of the animals. By 1914 there were six in the country. John Grayson (eighty), of Wombwell worked at Mitchell Main Colliery in the early 1920s and he said: "Some miners would fake accidents in order to get rid of a lazy pony. Their wages depended on how many tubs they filled and the speed with which they were taken to the shaft. They made sure the accident killed the pony. There was never an inquiry, the ponies were just written off. Hard working men and hard working ponies – that's what it was like for both man and beast down a pit." Mr Grayson, a farmer's son, quickly built up a relationship with his pony, Boxer. As a lad he picked the best grasses and carrots and took them to work to treat his pal. Despite such generosity, Boxer, like a good union man, knew his rights and when Grayson tried to persuade him to stay behind to enable the lad to earn some overtime Boxer refused and marched off to the stables. Boxer had his own internal clock and he knew what time his shift ended.

Sometimes ponies had their revenge. Tom, a pony at Monk Bretton Colliery, was said to have killed his driver in 1914. The inquest was told that a fifteen-year old boy was found dead behind a stationary Tom, with blood gushing from a wound in the head. The pony was said to be nasty when whipped but the lad, named Copley, was new to the job and did not know.

In 1913 more than 74,000 horses were at work but by 1947 the figure had dropped to 23,000; in the late 1970s there were still a few ponies, mainly in the North East.

BARNSLEY
PIT PONY & HORSE SHOW,

✦PRIZES.✦

COMPETITION 1.

The best Horse 14 hands or over.—1st Prize, £3 ; 2nd, £2 ; 3rd, £1.

The best Pony 12 hands and under 14.—1st Prize, £3 ; 2nd, £2 ; 3rd, £1.

The best Pony under 12 hands.—1st Prize, £3 ; 2nd, £2 ; 3rd, £1.

COMPETITION 2.

The best Horse or Pony certified to have worked in a Pit more than six years.—1st Prize, £3 ; 2nd, £2 ; 3rd, £1.

The best Horse or Pony certified to have worked in a Pit more than ten years.—First Prize, £3 ; 2nd, £2 ; 3rd, £1.

The Horse or Pony that has been working in a Pit the longest period.—1st Prize, £3 ; 2nd, £2 ; 3rd, £1.

COMPETITION 3.

A group of Horses or Ponies.

In a Colliery where more than 50 Horses and Ponies are employed, six animals must be shewn.

In a Colliery where there are less than 50 and more than 30 Horses and Ponies employed, four animals must be shewn.

In a Colliery where less than 30 Horses and Ponies are employed, two animals must be shewn.

Half the animals must be selected by the Proprietors and half by the Committee by lot (see Rules).

1st Prize, £5 ; 2nd, £3 ; 3rd, £2.

COMPETITION 4.

There will also be a Prize awarded to the Pit which exhibits their animals in the best condition in the Pit.

Some one or two persons will be chosen by the Committee, who will during the months of June and July visit each Pit competing, at a time convenient to the Manager, but without notice as to the particular day.

On such visit every animal in the Pit must be shewn.

1st Prize, £5 ; 2nd, £3 ; 3rd, £2.

No entry fee is chargeable for the last competition. In all other classes 1s. entry fee for each animal must be paid, and from this fund refreshments will be provided for the persons in charge of the animals.

The Prizes will be distributed among the Drivers and Horse-keepers.

No person but the Judges and the person or persons having charge of the animals will be allowed in the Show-Ring on any pretext, unless asked to come in by the Judges.

Wharncliffe Silkstone
Colliery, Tankersley:
Right: The blacksmith
shop.
Below: Repairing wagons.

Above: Pit top scene at Wharncliffe Silkstone.

Left: The weigh cabin at Wharncliffe Silkstone.

Above: The laboratory, Wharncliffe Silkstone.

Below: The by-product plant at Wharncliffe Silkstone.

Left: The lamp room at Monckton Colliery, Royston.
John Goodchild Collection.

Below: The lamp room at Wharncliffe Silkstone.
All the Wharncliffe Silkstone photographs loaned by Mrs G.A. Greaves, Wombwell.

RESCUE TEAMS

The first central rescue station was built at Tankersley in 1902 as a result of a Royal Commission in 1886 which recommended their establishment. Most of the later stations were built following the 1911 Mines Act with money provided by Coal Owners Associations or jointly by colliery companies.

Mr. G. V. Jolliffe, District Rescue Stations manager (Yorkshire District), in "The Changing Role of the Mines Rescue Service," said that with very little else to go on, fire brigades and the armed forces provided the ideas of establishment, and many of the stations reflected the designs of fire stations of the period. Most of the rescue officers had a background of fire station or armed forces service. The discipline and ethics of the service - even the uniforms of today were relics of the period.

"In those days the main attribute of the rescue man was an intense dedication to duty coupled with long mining experience, which meant that the teams included many older men. Superhuman tasks and long hours of duty were required of them. The science and technology of the rescue equipment itself, and the nature of gas emissions, and other disasters, was not so well understood in those days. Indeed, neither were the medical and human aspects of rescue work. As a result, nationally 34 members of the rescue service lost their lives between 1908 and 1962, many of them in the 55-65 age group."

Disasters occurred with alarming frequency - Gresford in 1934 (265 killed), Sneyd in 1942 (57), William Colliery in 1947 (104), Creswell in 1950 (80), Easington in 1951 (81) and Knockshinnoch in 1950, when 129 men were trapped by liquid peat.

Mr. Jolliffe said on nationalisation the committees were replaced by the NCB equivalent, with a local senior official as chairman. The modern service began to take shape from a reorganisation in 1967. He said:" A popular fallacy is that we spend our time rescuing people. This is not so because the people we are infrequently called upon to rescue have either got the hell out of it by their own efforts or are unfortunately already dead. The Houghton Main incident (1975) was a striking exception to this pattern in that the rescue team recovered a survivor from the disaster area."

As well as breathing apparatus, the stations have explosion-proof access tubes and other fittings necessary in the erection of stoppings, fire fighting equipment including protective clothing; wrecking and cutting tools to gain access to fire and accident sites; emergency lighting equipment; portable generators and portable radios.

The Lofthouse incident, when water flooded part of the workings, demonstrated the need for underwater rescue techniques. Some stations have special teams of rescue personnel trained in underwater techniques and equipped with the latest aqua-lung apparatus.

TWO TRAGEDIES

Seventy-seven men died in two explosions in the mid-1930s, nineteen at North Gawber Colliery in 1935 and fifty-eight at Wharncliffe Woodmoor 1,2,3 at Carlton in the following year.

At North Gawber a large pocket of methane gas ignited in the 4 South Face on September 12. More than thirty men were working on the afternoon shift when a hot blast swept down the face. As the dust and debris settled, those who could pick themselves up saw that fifteen of their colleagues were dead and

Above: Arthur Hatcher was awarded the Edward Medal in recognition of his heroism in saving the lives of four men by stopping a runaway tub at Barnsley Main Colliery in October, 1922. He stopped the tub within ten yards of three men who were helping a sick man. Mr Hatcher, Worsbrough Common, sustained serious back injuries.

Below Left: Old Carlton Pit Rescue Team, 1920s.
Mr D. Harley, Barnsley.

that a dozen others were injured, some of them severely. The power was switched off to avert another explosion. After a call was made for volunteers to try a rescue attempt, 4,000 relatives, sweethearts and friends gathered at the pithead, surging forward as each rescue team went underground. The Mayor of Barnsley, Alderman B.F. Canter, spent many hours at the pithead and said: "They asked for ten rescuers and you should have seen the rush the men made for the cages. Many in their best suits surged forward rolling up their sleeves and casting away cigarettes and matches, eager to go below and face the unknown dangers. They were magnificent." At the inquest Dr R. Millar said all but one of the men were badly burnt and showed signs of carbon monoxide poisoning. A witness said the men had been laughing and joking on the face when there was a sudden gust of wind. The inquest was told of the heroism of Mr Jim Crow, a young overman who was twenty yards from the explosion. Avoiding serious injury he managed to drag two injured miners, Walter Riley and Claude Ackroyd, to safety, although both died later in

hospital. He said: "I told Ackroyd to hang onto my clogs as I crawled along. The men were in a bad condition and the air was bad until we got to the middle gate where it became clearer."

The inquiry accepted that a build-up of gas had arisen and that because of poor ventilation the explosive mixture had been allowed to gather until it was too late. The inquiry criticised the mining company for allowing too many shots to be fired. The disaster scarred Mrs D. Woodruff, Springfield Road, Hoyland Common, for many years. Her father was Mr Riley, aged fifty-two, of Bridge Street, Darton, who left eight orphans. Mrs Woodruff was fifteen and after the explosion she had to collect £5 every month to keep the younger ones. "Had it not been for the disaster relief fund, we would have starved because the older ones did not have enough money to help out," she said. Her father had been complaining about the presence of gas for months before the explosion.

The explosion at Wharncliffe Woodmoor, caused by an electrical fault, occurred in the Lidgett seam at about four am on August 6, 1936. Fifty-seven men

Above: This team had just spent eight hours tackling a fire underground at Wharncliffe Woodmoor 1,2,3 Colliery, in the 1920s. The men, all deputies, were **left to right:** Instructor Mr Parkinson, Walter Trimby, William Turton, Jack Elrin, Sam Dutton. Mr Trimby, aged 40, died soon afterwards.

Wharncliffe Woodmoor 1,2,3 at Carlton. Viewed from the Royston end.

Right: Map used by newspaper to pinpoint the colliery after the explosion.

Below: New Carlton Colliery (later Wharncliffe Woodmoor 4/5.)

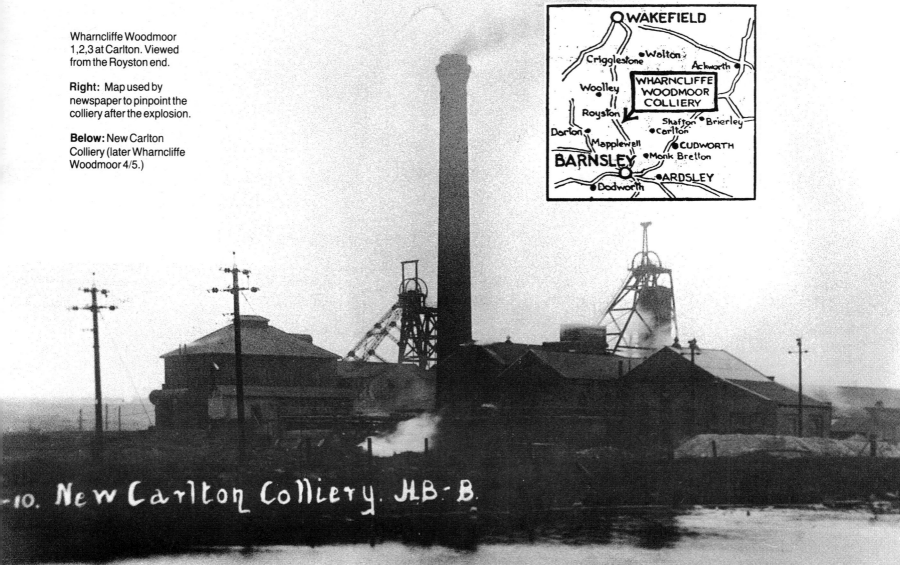

-10. New Carlton Colliery. H.B. B.

were killed outright, and the attendant of the haulage gear, Alfred Brown, was the sole man to be brought out alive but died five days later in hospital. It was said two airway doors had been wedged open with bricks by men taking tubs to and fro, resulting in the ventilation procedures failing to work properly, and firedamp accumulated on the face. The cover of the loader was found to be on the floor and the cover of the electrical starting switch was loose. The presence of combustible material was said to be a contributory factor: 201 tons of limestone had been sent to the pit over the previous seven months, and much of that was said to be combustible. At the inquiry, the Yorkshire Miners Association was represented by the president, Herbert Smith, who said it was his seventy-third experience of a mining disaster, the worst since Gresford two years earlier. Several women, after answering questions on the witness stand, almost collapsed under the strain and were assisted from the stand by nurses.

All Barnsley and its districts were in mourning. Blinds were drawn, flags on the buildings were flown at half mast and weeping men and women lined the road to Monk Bretton Cemetery on the day thirteen of the victims were buried. Scores of miners, friends of the victims, followed the coffins. At the graveside mothers, wives and sweethearts wept. They were, in almost every case, supported by uniformed nurses.

In 1979 Yorkshire miners' president Arthur Scargill unveiled a plaque in memory of the men who died in the disaster on a site off Laithes Lane. The inscription reads: "On the 6th August, 1936, a firedamp explosion caused by an electrical fault engulfed all face workers at Wharncliffe Woodmoor Colliery. There were no survivors: fifty-seven men died instantly − one survivor died later in hospital. This plaque commemorates the sacrifice underground." In his speech Mr Scargill said very few families in the

Above: Men pictured at Wharncliffe Woodmoor. *Yorkshire Mining Museum.*

Left: Long Carlton Row where many of the Wharncliffe Woodmoor men lived.

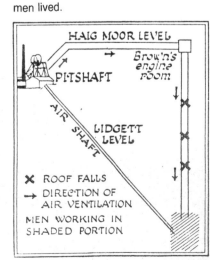

Plan of the workings of the colliery, showing in the shaded portions where the explosion occurred.

News Chronicle

ZIXT 4d

ONE PENNY — POSTAGE IN U.K., CANADA, AND NEWFOUNDLAND... 1d. Other Places Abroad 1½d.

FRIDAY, AUGUST 7, 1936

25 STILL MISSING IN WRECKED PIT

Rescuers Find 32 Bodies: One Man Survives

DOCTORS GIVE UP RESCUE HOPE

Gas Sweeps Through Blocked Workings

F. POLLARD,
...SLEY, Thursday

...with stretchers climbing to the pit cage to bring up the bodies of the victims.

POWERS AND SPAIN

...NCH ANXIETY

Chaos At Berlin Olympics

Organisation of the Berlin Olympic Games went to pieces yesterday.

In one event in which the gold medallist was a French man, the announcer gave the name of an Icelander and the audience stood up and salute... while the Icelandic Anthe... was played.

Later the Frenchman... brought out, and with any explanation t... "Marseillaise" was play...

The Nazi official newspa... "Angriff" is angry ove... success of negroes in... Games. "But for Ame... black auxiliary tribes... says, "the United... would have put up a... show."

MOTHER AND SO... TOGETHER

A five-years-old child an... were killed and the wom... was seriously injured wh... cycle combination on wh... riding came into colli... motor-coach at Horley... night.

Mrs. Edith Burgess, o... Poplar, E., and her son... victims. Mr. Albert... lett-road, Bow, the dri... cycle, was taken to He...

LATE

The Leeds Mercury

No. 30,169 —ESTABLISHED 1718.

An All-Yorkshire Journal and a Power in the North for More Than Two Hundred Years.

FRIDAY, AUGUST 7, 1936

DAILY—ONE PENN...

32 BODIES TAKEN FROM PIT.

Yorkshire Death-Roll 57.

ONE SURVIVOR OF EXPLOSION.

Hopes of Waiting Women Gone.

A MESSAGE FROM THE KING.

YORKSHIRE WAS STRICKEN YESTERDAY BY A TERRIBLE MINING DISASTER IN WHICH 57 MEN LOST THEIR LIVES.

THEY WERE VICTIMS OF AN EXPLOSION (BRIEFLY REPORTED IN A SPECIAL LATE EDITION OF YESTERDAY'S "MERCURY") AT THE WHARN-CLIFFE WOODMOOR COLLIERY, ROYSTON, NEAR BARNSLEY. EARLY THIS MORNING 32 BODIES HAD BEEN BROUGHT TO THE SURFACE. WORKERS IN THE MINE HAD A HARD TASK TO HEW THEIR WAY TO THE VICTIMS.

ONE man alone lived through the explosion. He is Alfred Brown, of Long Row, Smithies, who, though working nearly a mile away from the centre of the explosion, was terribly burned.

...tors and nurses were fighting for his life in Barnsley Hospital, but though his grave condition slightly improved, he remained unconscious. By his side waited his widowed mother.

...explosion occurred about 3.30 a.m. yesterday, in the Lidgett ...eam, about one and a half miles from the foot of the main shaft, ...a depth of over half a mile.

Moving Scenes at Pithead.

Women Who Waited.

From a "Mercury" Special Correspondent.

BARNSLEY, Thursday Night.
THERE were deeply moving scenes to-night when bodies of the dead in the Wharncliffe Wood-moor Colliery explosion were brought to the surface.

As the bodies were being taken by ambulance to a neighbouring school building, a woman's cry rose above the subdued murmurs. She had identified her husband.

The only thing she saw as the stretcher passed was his boot projecting beyond the blanket, but she said she knew that it was his. Only that morning her husband had wanted his boot eased for him. He could not get it on, he said, and she had cut the boot for him.

By that last service to her husband, she was able to identify him long before official identification took place.

READY FOR CARNIVAL.

One of the trapped men was to have been in Royston Carnival, and one of his three daughters had her gypsy costume ready for the event when the tragic news of the disaster reached their home.

The family was looking forward to a well-earned holiday with relatives in Liverpool. The wife was still hoping late to-night even after rescue parties had warned the crowd to abandon hope.

"It queer how often these things com... near holidays," someone remarked.

READY TO RISK THEIR LIVES.—Rescue workers did valiant work in the disaster at Wharncliffe Woodmoor Colliery. Here is a rescue party. (By a "Mercury" photographer.)

RELIEF FUND TO BE OPENED.

Mr. Joseph Jones Coming Home.

From Our Correspondent.
BARNSLEY, Thursday Night.
THE Deputy Mayor of Barnsley, Alderman B. F. Canter, who visited the Wharncliffe Wood-moor Colliery during the day, has decided to open a relief fund in the town. Mr. Joseph...

LIST OF THE VICTIMS.

THE list of 57 men believed to have perished as a result of the Wharncliffe Woodmoor Colliery disaster is printed below.

Alfred Brown, of Long Row, Smithies, is in hospital suffering from injuries.

George FARMERY, deputy, 20, Tempest Avenue, Darfield.
Joseph H. HOPE, deputy, 30, Mottram Street, Barnsley.
Wm. O. TOMPKINS, packer, 54, Park Road, Worsborough Bridge.
Richard B. GRIMSHAW, dataller, 56, Smithies Lane, Barnsley.
Victor CLARKSON, machine man, 50, Birkwood Avenue, Cudworth.
Samuel BROWN, machine man, 14, Murton Road, Burton, Barnsley.
Ernest DALBY, machine man, 51, Priory Road, Lundwood, Barnsley.
Henry BIRKHEAD, ripper...

Frank COOPER, ripper, Sheffield Road, Barnsley.
Richard WRIGHT, ripper, 7, Gray's Road, Carlton.
Arthur HAIGH, machine man, 5, Richard St., Barnsley.
C. E. ISMAY, machine man, Broadway New Road, Smithies.
James GREEN, ripper, 1, Allendale Road, Darton West.
J. W. H. ABBOTT, ripper, Willow Bank, Smithies.
S. KIRK, ripper, 66, Wakefield Road, Smithies.
Henry WRIGHT, ripper, 24, John Edward Street, Barnsley.
John ROSCOE, dataller, 41, Bedford Terrace, Wakefield Road, Smithies.
Herbert HAL...

NY OTHER BREAD
once you've tasted
DON'
nshine Milk Bread

Daily Independent

No. 25,519—Founded 1819

TELEPHONE NOS.: EDITORIAL, Sheffield 24051; ADVERTISING, COMMERCIAL, Etc. 24351

SHEFFIELD, FRIDAY, 7 AUGUST, 1936

2   ONE PENNY

LATE CITY EDITION

BROADCAST PROGRAMM

When it comes to
Mind — you don

Bear Br
Hose behin

All Hope Abandoned in Barnsley Pit Explosion
THIRTY-THREE BODIES RECOVERED
ONLY ONE OF 58 MEN BROUGHT OUT ALIVE
Relatives Collapse Under Ordeal in Schoolroom Mortuary

E KING'S
SYMPATHY

E KING, last night, sent the
ollowing message to Lord
wood, Lord-Lieutenant for
West Riding:—

'am greatly distressed to
of the accident at the
ncliffe Woodmoor Colliery,
the serious loss of life
red.   Please convey my
sympathy to the bereaved
es and my best wishes to
ured for a quick recovery."
hall be glad to hear how the
work progresses. (Signed)
d R.I."

Harewood replied:—
r Majesty's sympathetic
e shall be conveyed to the
s of the sufferers. I am
d there is very slight hope
e loss of life will be less
ty-seven."

rds Meant
e to These
tan Wives

NSTANCE LISTER

got to be brave to wed

of the words of an old
shire miner's wife as
h the crowd keeping
rain.   People talked
A shawl fell to the
a little old woman near
beat on her head.
own," she said. Nothing
was a little rustle as
towards her. No one
mean little to the spartan
s.
here hot tea was being
Salvation Army sat a
nths, the wife of Arthur

ALL hope of rescuing alive any of the 57 men entombed in the Wharncliffe Woodmoor Colliery, near Barnsley, had last night been virtually abandoned.

By shortly after midnight 33 bodies had been recovered, and rescue parties suspended operations until 6 a.m.

One man alone lived through the horror of the disastrous explosion. If the story of the swift, devastating minute of death and destruction is ever told, he alone can tell it.

That man is Alfred Brown, who, though working three-quarters of a mile away from the centre of the explosion, was terribly burned and shocked.

Last night doctors and nurses were fighting for his life in Barnsley Hospital—he had earlier been reported dead. Though his condition had slightly improved, he remained unconscious. By his side waited his widowed mother.

It is the worst British mine disaster since September, 1934, when 265 men were killed in the Gresford Colliery.

RESCUE WORK SUSPENDED

by the block in the roads and the breaking down of ventilation doors owing to the violence of the explosion allowed icy cold air to sweep through the working at a terrific rate. There could be no rest for the rescue workers in such conditions.

MEMBERS OF THE RESCUE TEAMS who descended Wharncl
Woodmoor Pit after the explosion are seen above and on le
(More pictures on Back Page.)

DAILY INDEPENDENT PHOTOGR

Olympic Games
British Runner Sets Up New World Record
By W. CAPEL KIRBY

BERLIN, Thursday.

BRITISH flags were unfurled and run to the top of th Olympic mast to-day. Twice we joined in the lust singing of "God Save the King," while 110,000 people stoo stiffly to attention, the majority of them giving the Hitle salute.

It was a proud moment for our small British contin

for Harold Whitlock and Jack Lovelock, to whom

surrounding areas were not affected, directly or indirectly, by the explosion in 1936. "It is the price that we have to pay for the coal we need. The town has been built on coal. Many thousands of people owe their lives to the mining industry, and it is right and proper that we should remember this terrifying experience all those years ago."

The memorial, designed in the form of a pithead wheel mounted vertically on a stone plinth, was the idea of the late Councillor Harry Dancer, who felt a memorial should be erected in memory of the men. The oldest man at the ceremony was eighty-five years old Charles Hardcastle, of Carlton, who said: "If it had happened on another shift, hundreds would have been killed."

After nearly sixty years an incident can stir old memories. When there was a public outcry against the closure of thirty-one pits in October, 1992, the Chronicle received the following letter from A. Marsland, of Darton: "I have felt the urge to write a story of a simple mining family. My grandfather, Lewis Boyd, worked at Wharncliffe Woodmoor Colliery — he had a son William at the same pit and my father was at North Gawber. One day William went to work his first shift at the mine and never came back — he

was killed in the pit cage. Six months later my grandfather went to work at Wharncliffe Woodmoor and was killed in the disaster. My father went with the rescue team to look for his father but couldn't find him. "Have you seen my husband?" asked a neighbour. "No, lass," he said. How could he tell her that he had seen him hanging upside down without his legs. Later they found my grandfather — without a mark on him — trapped behind some air doors. Some years later when I was a child the pit van pulled up outside the gate and the driver got out with a bundle of clothes tied up with a belt — you can imagine what state my mother was in. "Don't worry, lass, he isn't bad," said the driver. That day or two ran into weeks and my father's back was like a map of England with all the holes and scars and he was in pain until his death last November at the age of eighty-one. Michael Heseltine says he feels pain at what he had to do; it's not pain but guilt. Pain is when a mother is told her husband or father is dead, or when a wife is told her husband is in hospital and won't be the same again. Will anyone remember Michael Heseltine with pride?"

Above and Left:
Newspapers dealing with the 1936 explosion. "Tha's got to be brave to wed a miner" poignant words—see left hand column above.

Below: A party of rescue workers going to the pithead.

Above: The rescue team.

Right: The Salvation Army hand out cups of tea.

Left: The Earl of Wharncliffe walking down the colliery yard.

Right: Barnsley MP Mr J. Potts (left) talking at the pithead.

Below Left: Rescue workers with a pit canary which they took underground to warn them of gas.

PIT PHONE CALLS FOR AMBULANCE

me that all the damage y. The other way or the e said, was absolutely.

 all I came to," he said, ..200 yards from the face t seam." re lots of other falls after ." said this rescue worker then he added: "All I can here had been a bad bump."

V WAS SAVED

e words a man who had faced ry to reach the entombed men s experiences.

Above: A stretcher case.

Left: The mortuary at Carlton school.

93

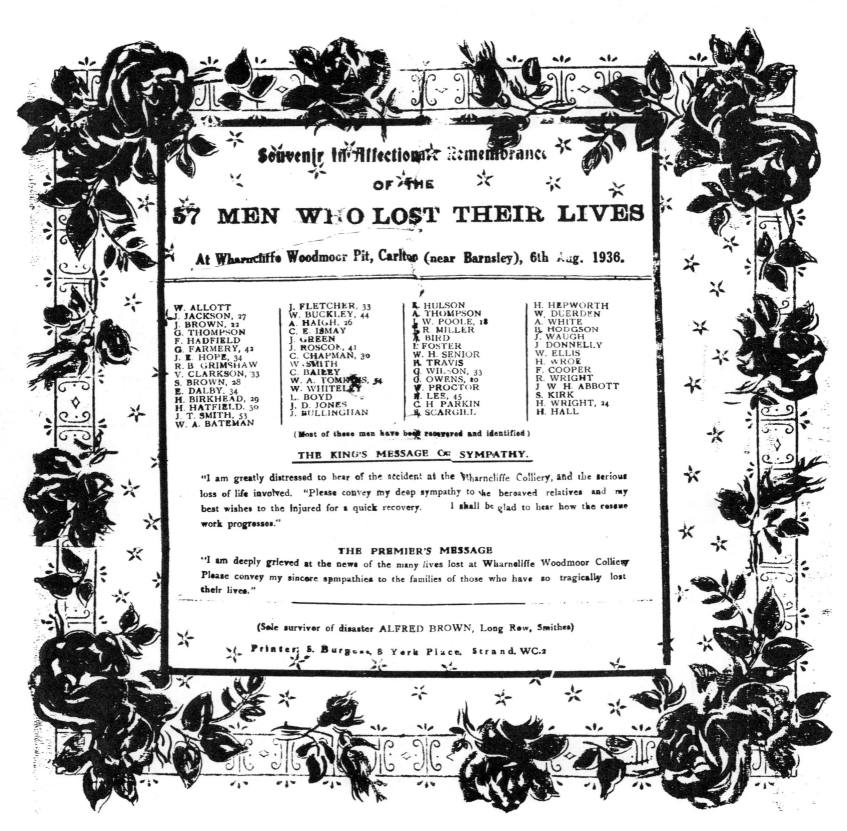

Souvenir In Affectionate Remembrance

OF THE

57 MEN WHO LOST THEIR LIVES

At Wharncliffe Woodmoor Pit, Carlton (near Barnsley), 6th Aug. 1936.

W. ALLOTT	J. FLETCHER, 33	E. HULSON	H. HEPWORTH
J. JACKSON, 27	W. BUCKLEY, 44	A. THOMPSON	W. DUERDEN
J. BROWN, 22	A. HAIGH, 26	W. POOLE, 18	A. WHITE
G. THOMPSON	C. E. ISMAY	R. MILLER	B. HODGSON
F. HADFIELD	J. GREEN	A. BIRD	J. WAUGH
G. FARMERY, 42	J. ROSCOE, 41	I. FOSTER	J. DONNELLY
J. E. HOPE, 34	C. CHAPMAN, 30	W. H. SENIOR	W. ELLIS
R. B. GRIMSHAW	W. SMITH	R. TRAVIS	H. WROE
V. CLARKSON, 33	C. BAILEY	G. WILSON, 33	F. COOPER
S. BROWN, 28	W. A. TOMKINS, 54	G. OWENS, 20	R. WRIGHT
E. DALBY, 34	W. WHITELEY	V. PROCTOR	J W H. ABBOTT
H. BIRKHEAD, 29	L. BOYD	R. LEE, 45	S. KIRK
H. HATFIELD, 30	J. D. JONES	C H PARKIN	H. WRIGHT, 24
J. T. SMITH, 53	J. BULLINGHAN	R. SCARGILL	H. HALL
W. A. BATEMAN			

(Most of these men have been recovered and identified)

THE KING'S MESSAGE OF SYMPATHY.

"I am greatly distressed to hear of the accident at the Wharncliffe Colliery, and the serious loss of life involved. "Please convey my deep sympathy to the bereaved relatives and my best wishes to the injured for a quick recovery. I shall be glad to hear how the rescue work progresses."

THE PREMIER'S MESSAGE

"I am deeply grieved at the news of the many lives lost at Wharncliffe Woodmoor Colliery. Please convey my sincere sympathies to the families of those who have so tragically lost their lives."

(Sole survivor of disaster ALFRED BROWN, Long Row, Smithes)

Printer: S. Burgess, 8 York Place, Strand. WC.2

A napkin produced to mark the 1936 disaster.

Chapter 4

1940-1970 War and Nationalisation

Below: Gedney's private mine at Hemingfield.
R.J. Short/G. Beedan.

The industry did a somersault during the Second World War. The owners, ascendant after the crushing defeat of the miners in 1926, lost control of the pits in the war and then became an extinct species after 1947. The union, disunited and disheartened between the wars, became a unified powerful body in 1945 with the formation of the National Union of Mineworkers.

At the beginning of the war, in 1939, the pits were in the hands of a multitude of companies, with the number of directors running into several thousand. The companies owned 2,000 mines, with 700,000 men on the books, 300,000 fewer than in the early 1920s. Output per man improved between the wars but the technical standards could not compete with those in America and Germany. One expert, speaking on the television programme, *All Our Working Lives*, in 1993, said the high productivity levels in Germany before the war were due to superior haulage systems – which moved the coal to the shaft faster and in greater quantity than the British systems – whereas there was little to choose between the calibre of equipment on the coal faces in both countries. He also believed the narrow roadways in UK pits would have been unsuitable for the German-style haulage systems. Others disagreed, believing that the problem was much deeper and wider and that Britain lagged behind other countries in the mechanisation stakes. Another former pit manager, on the same programme, said there had been in the 1930s a widespread belief that nationalisation of the pits was inevitable and there was a reluctance by management to spend money on an asset which would end up in the hands of the Government in the long term.

As the war approached one chronic problem started to disappear, the dole queue, which had bedevilled the 1920s and 1930s. Within weeks of the outbreak of war there was a chronic shortage of workers in the mines. In the first three weeks 23,000 miners followed the example of their fathers or uncles in the First World War and enlisted. The Government demanded an increase in production from 260 to 270 million tons per year but output fell sharply between 1939 and 1942, and dual control of the pits was introduced: policy was laid down by the Government and the pit manager remained

Left: Wharncliffe Woodmoor 4/5 before and after nationalisation.
Lord Mason.

95

Above: Elsecar Main, 1940s.

Right: Broomhill football team, 1940s. Miners were highly skilled footballers (see Men of Iron).
Alf Jones (standing, second right)

in the employment of the owner. As production fell, absenteeism reared its ugly head, as it had done in the First World War. The public blamed absenteeism for all the ills in the pits. In defence, Mr Joe Hall, president of the Yorkshire miners, said: "A man must be perfectly fit when going down the pit. Ours is an industry where nature has never been kind to us, and never will be. Ours is an industry in regard to which the finest experts and the best mining engineers have never been able to quantify the facts that govern it. Impeded production can take place because of many things: bad roadways and bad ventilation, and our men have to suffer these continued abnormalities and excessive pressures." In reality the pits were ill equipped to cope with a wartime economy because in the 1930s investment had lagged behind that of our competitors.

In 1943 Mr Ernest Bevin, the Minister of Labour and National Service, worried by the shortage of mineworkers, spent more than £20,000 on advertising nationwide to try to fill the vacancies and some 3,000 responded. Dissatisfied with the response the Government introduced conscription with one out of ten being directed into the mines instead of the armed forces, the famous "Bevin Boys." Meanwhile the owners put forward proposals to reorganise the industry; their chief spokesman was the Prime Minister, Mr Winston Churchill, who had called the miners "the enemy" in the 1920s. Their proposals had come too late, many believed, because there should have been reorganisation in the early 1930s with the emphasis on amalgamated and modern companies with improved marketing, a suggestion resisted by some owners at the time. Counter proposals were submitted by the unions: they had been badgering for nationalisation since the 1880s without any success. The landslide victory by the Labour Party in 1945 clinched the issue with the electorate demanding a fresh start in the nation with new ideas and institutions; this time there would be no return to the bad old days, the nation declared.

The pits were nationalised in January, 1947, and within four weeks the country was hit by a disastrous fuel shortage. The bleak winter, during which more than a million men were out of work because factories had to close, was the moment at which the Conservatives realised Labour was not invincible; at the same time the public turned on the old bogeymen, the miners. It was unfair of the public to blame the miners for failing to cut enough coal. Had there been adequate stocks, the railways would have been incapable of moving supplies around the country. Speaking in the 1970s, Lord Shinwell, the former Minister of Power, said of that winter: "We had all sorts of problems: shortage of miners, shortage of coal, shortage of railway wagons, and on top of that serious weather — perhaps the worst weather we have had for many years." Lord Robens, later chairman of the NCB, said: "I think the real cause of the 1947 fuel crisis was the abnormal weather coupled with the fact there was an overall shortage of coal." Too much or too little coal: the mining industry never got it right at the right time.

In the early 1950s the board stepped up mechanisation and pits were given face-lifts and by the late 50s full mechanisation, using the shearer-loader which put coal on the conveyor belt, was in general use. The unions and the public had been blaming the owners for inadequate investment for years before nationalisation; now was the time for action, declared the Government, and money was poured down the shafts. Whereas there

Left: A typical scene in the 1930s and 1940s. Coal picking at Darfield.
R.J. Short/Cusworth Museum.

Above: Hemsworth
Colliery: full side pit bottom.

had been a coal famine in 1947, there was a glut of coal a few years later, thanks to higher productivity, and to add to the problems of the pits industries were changing over to cheap oil. More pithead baths were built and mobile x-ray units introduced. Miners, particularly face workers, prospered and by the mid and late 1950s a face-worker could earn £20 per week for a five-day week, putting them at the top of the blue collar wages league, a marked contrast to the earnings in the 1930s. Miners started to buy their homes and cars were no longer a middle class status symbol, even if most of their vehicles were second hand. The first cracks were appearing in what had been traditional mining communities, close-knit communities where everyone knew everyone else and where leisure and pastimes were centred on the street or a group of streets, and work meant the pit at the bottom of the hill. High disposable income and the motor car, television and holidays abroad did more over the next three decades to destroy the old patterns and spirit in the villages than all the Conservative Governments have alleged to have done. On the industrial relations front in the 1950s Yorkshire was plagued by petty and unofficial strikes. Often they were caused by friction between deputies, the old enemy who took the flak on the coal face, and miners. For example,

deputies were in the invidious position of having to determine special payments to miners; the managers sometimes overruled them and when miners opened their wage packets there was uproar. Public opinion had been turning against miners for some years, for nationalisation had promised too much and delivered too little as far as they were concerned. The public had expected improved productivity and fewer strikes; productivity increased, as did wages, but industrial relations did not change (one old miner said the pits had been nationalised but the bosses were still the same).

Lord Robens resigned from Parliament in 1961 to become chairman of the National Coal Board, a post he held until 1971 when he resigned over the Government's failure to run the industry like a business. During his term of office 400 pits were closed and one job in two, 300,000 in all, disappeared. It was the age of the axeman. Lord Beeching, chairman of British Rail, cut the railways down to size, Lord Robens wielded the axe on the pits. His reign resulted in a 50 per cent increase in productivity and he also managed to keep a lid on pay rises, although that stoked up trouble for the future when miners realised they were falling behind other workers. According to Lord Robens, two new

REPORT

AND

GENERAL STATEMENTS

OF

OAKS COLLIERY

EXPLOSION RELIEF FUND

FOR THE

Year ending 30th June, 1950.

Barnsley :

R. E. GRIFFITHS LTD., PRINTERS, HANSON STREET.

—

1950.

The Oaks Colliery Explosion Relief Fund.

REPORT 30th JUNE, 1950.

The Dependents on the Fund at the present time number 19, divided into the following Classes :—

	Men.	Women	Children.	Total.	Weekly Relief	Total per annum. £ s. d.
Swaithe Main Volunteer	1	...	...	1	@ 15/-	39 0 0
Wharncliffe Silkstone Widow	...	1	...	1	@ 15/-	39 0 0
Wath Main Widows ...	...	2	...	2	@ 15/-	78 0 0
Houghton Main Widow	...	1	...	1	@ 15/-	39 0 0
Cortonwood Widows ...	...	2	...	2	@ 15/-	78 0 0
Upton Main Widows ...	...	3	...	3	@ 15/-	117 0 0
,, ,, Orphan ...	...	...	1	1	@ 15/-	39 0 0
Manvers Main Widow	...	1	...	1	@ 15/-	39 0 0
North Gawber Widows	...	7	...	7	@ 10/.	182 0 0
				19		£650 0 0

The 7 remaining Widows of the North Gawber Disaster, 1935, have been granted relief from 18th March, 1950, at the rate of 10/- per week each.

The following 3 Dependents have died during the year, viz :—

James Hawkins, Swaithe Main Volunteer ;

Samuel Snidall,   do.

Mildred Landles, Cortonwood Widow.

The Income of the Fund during the year was £760 9s. 0d. and the Expenditure £641 11s 7d

The Capital of the Fund invested with the Official Trustees of Charitable Funds is in :—

£25,348 8s. 3d. 3% Savings Bonds, 1965-75.

LIST OF DEPENDENTS ON FUND.

30th JUNE, 1950.

NAME.	ADDRESS	When put on Fund.	Age.
SWAITHE MAIN VOLUNTEER.			
Hammond, John ...	86, Wilthorpe Avenue, Barnsley	20 Jan., 1927	86
WHARNCLIFFE SILKSTONE WIDOW			
Gardner, Mrs. E. ...	32, Station Street, Swinton ...	23 July, 1938	75
WATH MAIN WIDOWS.			
Cusworth, Mrs. C. ...	12, Princess Street, West Melton ...	20 Jan., 1940	49
Unwin, Mrs. E. ...	6, Cawood Street, Mexbro'	20 Jan., 1940	64
HOUGHTON MAIN WIDOW.			
Lackey, Mrs. E. ...	10, Pitt Street, Low Valley ...	20 Jan., 1940	54
CORTONWOOD WIDOWS.			
Allen, Mrs. L. M. ...	41, Hoyle Mill Road, Stairfoot ...	27 July, 1940	65
Outram, Mrs. E. E.	14, Victoria Road, West Melton ...	27 July, 1940	60
UPTON MAIN WIDOWS.			
Overton, Mrs. L. ...	12, Twist Lane, Leigh, Lancs.	4 April, 1942	42
Dakin, Mrs. M. W. ...	63, Tam Wood, Ash Lane, Upton	4 April, 1942	49
Stevens, Mrs. D. ...	4, St. James Avenue, Ilkeston	4 April, 1942	58
UPTON MAIN ORPHAN.			
Rich, G. E. ...	c/o Mrs. Rich, 65, Harewood Lane, Upton	4 April, 1942	16

LIST OF DEPENDENTS ON FUND.—*Continued.*

NAME.	ADDRESS.	When put on Fund.	Age.
MANVERS MAIN WIDOW.			
Kelsey, Mrs. H. ...	2, Prince Street, Swinton ...	10 Aug., 1946	31
NORTH GAWBER WIDOWS.			
Bunting, Mrs. C. A.	7, Derwent Road, Ripley ...	18 March, 1950	66
Ibberson, Mrs. F. ...	14, South Street, Barnsley	18 March, 1950	55
Roberts, Mrs. E. ...	52, Wilthorpe Avenue, Barnsley	18 March, 1950	53
Senior, Mrs. E. A. ...	24, Spring Wood, New Mill ...	18 March, 1950	59
Walley, Mrs. D. ...	371, Higham Common Road. Higham ...	18 March, 1950	51
Whewall, Mrs. E. B.	9, Wright's Terrace, Barnsley	18 March, 1950	56
Harrison, Mrs. O. ...	13, Edward Street, Staincross	18 March, 1950	37

Above and Left: The 1950 Oaks Colliery explosion relief fund. Note that a survivor of the Swaithe Colliery disaster, aged 86, was still receiving relief.

problems emerged in the 1960s: cheap oil imports and the rise of the militant left in the NUM. He wrote: "One of the ridiculous aspects of the extreme left wing in trade unions has always been their enthusiasm for strikes, whereas in the Soviet Union and in the Iron Curtain countries strikes are illegal."

The miners felt threatened in the 1960s. It was the era of full employment and young men left the pits in droves believing it was a moribund industry: high wages could be earned elsewhere without the arduous work and car workers were seen as the elite workers. No longer were miners at the top of the wages league and coalfields like Barnsley were mangled in the pit closure programme. In Yorkshire the militants blamed the right wing leadership for failure to take a hard line against the NCB and the Government and it was clear that the discontent bubbling under the surface would boil over at sometime. The late 1960s saw the emergence of Arthur Scargill, then NUM delegate at Woolley Colliery, as a political figure. In 1966 at a special conference called to discuss the Labour Party's fuel policy, Scargill accused the NUM executive of failing to oppose the Labour Government's pit closure programme and argued against the closure of uneconomic pits. He called for an annual output of 200 million tons of coal. All the phrases have a familiar ring about them and nearly 30 years later he is still fighting a Government pit closure

programme. At the same time Scargill and a group of miners decided to change NUM policy and in 1967 the Yorkshire left formed the Miners' Forum. The one thing that marked him out from the rest was his youth – he was ten years younger than any other member. His face started appearing on regional television news programmes and his name in the provincial newspapers. He was a born PR man. Whereas the Yorkshire NUM leaders were rather aloof and sometimes inarticulate – the media is incapable of coming to terms with such figures – Arthur was always available for a crisp and rational quote to put some pep or venom into an otherwise staid newspaper story or television programme. It became easier for the Press to contact Arthur, still a pit delegate, than deal with the legitimate leadership who would mumble incoherent comments and release stories without a beginning and an end. Arthur's face beamed from the television sets, much to the annoyance of the older miners who thought him brash and too left wing. The old men remembered the 1920s and 1930s, the days when working men did what they were told. Arthur wasn't like the old union leaders and did not like being told what to do. He received more space in the newspapers and on television that his union post warranted. My old boss used to say: "He's only a pit delegate but he is talking as if he is the president of the Yorkshire miners."

By the late 1960s and early 1970s a groundswell of agitation was sweeping the coalfields in response to the fear that the miners were tumbling down the industrial wages ladder. With Scargill poised to become the union's Yorkshire compensation agent – the first step towards the Yorkshire leadership – the stage was set for the upheavals of the 1970s.

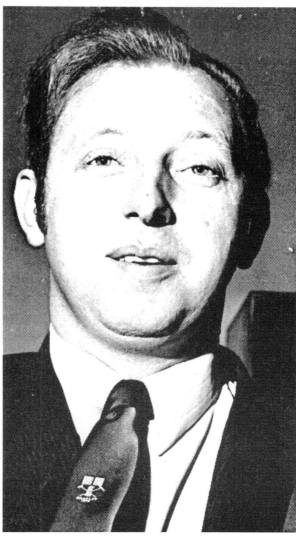

Opposite Page:
Hemsworth Colliery: 1949 and 1950.
Top Left: Middle ventilation gate/roadway on hand got coal face.
Middle Left: Rope-hauled paddy train
Bottom Left: The machine used to pull paddy train.

Left: Page 100: Advancing hand got longwall face with undercut machine at Hemsworth Colliery.

Hemsworth photographs loaned by J.B. Norton.

Above: Early type of armoured face conveyor. The photograph shows link type roof support bars and friction type legs.

Left: Arthur Scargill who made a name for himself in the 1960s.

101

BARNSLEY MAIN

Nine men were killed and twenty-one injured by a sheet of flame which swept through workings 720 feet below ground at Barnsley Main Colliery on Wednesday, May 7, 1947. The explosion, in number three district of the Kent Thick Seam, opened about a year earlier, occurred at about 12.15 pm shortly before the day workers were due to finish their shift. The disaster followed the nationalisation of the mines in January and the introduction of the five day week. Soon after the news had spread, wives and other relatives appeared at the scene and after the injured had been taken to hospital, stretchers bearing the dead were carried from the pithead to the first aid room which served as the mortuary.

Believed to have been caused by the sparking of an electric underground cable which in turn ignited dust, the explosion produced a sheet of flame but no fire. Survivors all spoke of a violent rush of air which hurled men six or eight yards and choking fumes. One rescue worker said: "Down there you could not tell there had been an explosion." Another rescue worker said all the bodies had been badly burned and all were killed instantly.

Mr Joe Hall, Yorkshire miners' president, said: "In thirty-six pit disasters I have experienced there has never been less trouble in getting men and getting them away to the first aid stations established at the pit bottom and on the surface. We found my old friend, Harry Storey, with whom I had worked on previous rescue jobs and who has done good work as a rescue team leader knocked out near the coal face. We carried him back and on the way I tried artificial respiration. At the pit bottom we all tried but he was dead before we got to the top." A tragic figure was the father of Harry Crowcroft. Though encased in a plaster cast as a result of an accident in which he had sustained injuries to his spine, he waited for news of his son. It was a distraught father who was led away when he was told his son had been killed. Members of Barnsley Main rescue team worked with the knowledge that one of their members was among the missing men. He was Mr Storey, shotfirer and deputy in charge, whose body was the last to be brought to the surface. Had he listened to his wife's pleas he would not have been at work, for he had been recovering from an earlier accident and had returned home the previous day feeling too sick to eat; he went to bed and was nursed by Mrs Storey, who begged him not to go to work on the fateful day.

There had been tragic events in the life of another victim, Harry Baxter. Suffering from a miners' knee complaint, he had been off work for a month and had restarted work on the Monday, and having found it too strenuous had been found lighter work; Wednesday was the first day in his new job.

The day before the explosion one of the victims had mentioned the presence of gas, the coroner, Mr S.H.B. Gill, was told at the inquest at Barnsley Town Hall. Mrs Storey said her husband said there had been gas in the pit and had arrived home feeling ill the day before the explosion. The jury returned a verdict of death by misadventure and the foreman juror, Mr H. Matthews, said the jury didn't know whether it was within their province but they thought there had been gross negligence in operating a machine without the cover which was supposed to prevent accidents. The explosion was caused by arcing from an electric cable and the jury felt the electric cable should have been examined at least once a shift by an electrician. And they also felt the ventilation door should have had a foundation. Mr Gill said a previous accident at the colliery had been caused by a trailing cable and when one considered the rough area over which the cable had to be hauled, it did seem important that they should be examined by someone with electrical knowledge. He said: "While there may have been a case of slight negligence in this case, I could not direct you that anyone has been neglectful in a criminal way."

Dr H. K. Willett, head of the Mines Rescue and Safety Department, North Eastern Division, said he considered it was not an explosion of great violence. He came to the conclusion that the explosion had been caused by an arc from the damaged cable igniting an explosive mixture of firedamp as it was emitted from the waste adjacent to the pan engine. The opening of the ventilation door by a surveying team caused gas to be moved towards the trailing cable.

Above: Barnsley Main which closed in the 1960s. *Barnsley Council's Local Studies Department.*

Left: Pictured examining their George Cross medals — special awards for bravery in civilian life — outside Buckingham Palace in December 1947 are Syd Blackburn (right) and Harry Crummack with their wives Norah and Annie. They were commended for their bravery after the explosion in May, 1947.

103

THE FIRST CRACKS

Like most people of my generation, I am ambivalent towards the 1950s, our childhood years. On one hand I believe that the quality of our family and community life deteriorated when we bought a television set and a new car in the mid 1950s, an unorthodox view in the 1990s when the world is dominated by the car and what people own; on the other hand, I have never known anyone who has wanted to go back to those days, even when they wallow in nostalgia about the old mining villages. But one thing can be certain — the first cracks appeared in the traditional close-knit mining communities in the 1950s.

Back in the 1950s the second social revolution was on its way. The first was the introduction of the welfare state which had exterminated the pests from the 1920s and 1930s, poverty and many childhood diseases; the second ushered in the age of the consumer with the result that miners, like other people in the country, changed their goals in life: television, property, consumer durables and holidays becoming all important. All helped to break down the old community spirit built up over four or five decades and which had focused on the premise that everyone was in the same boat. In that old world the men had

worked at the same pit, belonged in the main to the same union, read the same mass circulation newspapers, had the same pastimes and hobbies, most of which were centred on the village. The women did the same job – housework, a full time and arduous occupation – and shared the same female interests, and the children went to the same schools. Most of the families lived in two types of houses, the terraces where everyone lived on top of each other, knowing each other's business and listening to the domestic rows through paper-thin walls, or on council estates where there was at least some privacy. Apart from the occasional day trip and week's holiday at the seaside – almost all headed for the same resorts, Blackpool and Scarborough, in August – most of their lives were spent in the village. By and large the rest of the family lived nearby, providing support in times of emotional need. There was still a strong sense of the group, the last vestiges of the old tribal system.

Back in the 1950s and early 1960s it was still possible to find families who had lived in the same house for several generations and old people who had never been to the seaside. One of my colleagues said some of his relatives never seemed to leave the end of the street, rarely venturing into Barnsley; but once a year they ordered a taxi to take them to the railway station in Barnsley, en route to Blackpool where they spent a week by the sea, often bumping into their neighbours who had headed to the same destination. As children in the late 40s and early 50s we lived in a world within a world. Our back yard was one world and beyond the high brick walls surrounding the yard there was a far off world of which we knew little. We provided our own entertainment, most of which was centred on sport. In the summer cricket matches were organised between the families, with the oldest player in his late fifties and the youngest four or five years of age. The pitch was a short stretch of concrete in front of two

Above: Glamour was added to Yorkshire miners' galas in 1947. This line-up was photographed at Rotherham in the mid 1960s.

Left: Anderson-Boyes undercut machine for hand got face where coal is bored and fired before being filled out by hand. 1951.
J.B. Norton

houses or a rough piece of ground which became a dust bowl in hot weather. Soccer was reserved for the winter when players impersonating their league favourites slithered and tackled in the snow. It was an exhilerating and fun-laced world and at one point that yard ran its own athletic meetings, its own newspaper full of the mundane activities in that little world, its own children's library and its own children's plays, written in a cellar and performed in a garden. As the 50s progressed, however, disposable income increased and the inevitable arrival of televisions and cars broke down that bonhomie.

Local newspapers thrived on this kind of inward looking life. People in those days were more interested in news about the community and who had married and who had died. The newspaper circulations reflected this spirit: the *South Yorkshire Times* at Mexborough, which covered all the mining villages in the Dearne Valley, had a circulation of nearly 50,000 and the *Barnsley Chronicle* sold more than 40,000 per week. In the 1990s the South Yorkshire Times circulation has dipped to below 16,000 and the Chronicle's readership wavers between 37,000 and 40,000. Elsewhere, as in Doncaster, some weekly newspapers with robust circulations back in the 1950s and 1960s have disappeared. It is not so much that the newspapers have changed — the Chronicle's news stories in the main edition are very similar to the kind

printed 30 years ago — but the readers, whose horizons have widened: they move house more frequently than in the past — and as a consequence they do not know who lives down the same street — and have cars to take them beyond the town or village boundaries. Newspapers no longer have a monopoly on people's spare time; in the main people are too busy surviving or enjoying themselves to be bothered with what's going on round the corner. The pits which bound men together have gone, as have the factories which once employed a thousand or more workers. The men and women have other jobs, often work some miles away from their homes and spend their leisure time pursuing different pastimes to their neighbours. Holidays are often spent abroad, not in Blackpool which had been an annexe of Barnsley in the 1950s. These new influences were breaking down the pit communities long before the last mines disappeared.

The NUM may have said they were fighting to retain the old ways and values when they launched their campaign to save the thirty-one pits in October, 1992, but you have to go back to the early 1970s to find what a miner from an earlier era would have recognised as a prime example of a mining village, and even then he would have found much that had changed. The 1984/85 strike and the subsequent big shake-out of labour and pit closure programme sounded the death knell.

Right: The old Dearne and Dove canal and the Mexborough to Manchester railway line at Aldham, Wombwell. Mitchell Main colliery is in the background.
R. Firth, Wombwell.

Right: Wombwell Main shortly before closure.
R. Firth.

Left: Wombwell Main Colliery.
John Gill.

106

Right: Surface buildings at Wombwell Main.
R. Firth.

Below: Mr M. Greaves in the engine room.
R. Firth.

WINTER

S/WOOD

BEAMSHAW

BARNSLEY

Left: The end is in sight for Wombwell Main. An engine room attendant contemplates his future. *M. Firth.*

Below: Below the last shift finishes at Wombwell Main, May 23, 1969. *M. Firth.*

Above and Right: Demolition work at Wombwell Main.
R. Firth

Chapter 5
Victory and Decline

The miners swept through the country like a tidal wave in the 1970s and even 10 Downing Street was awash in 1974. Those national strike victories, coupled with a revitalised coal industry and rising income which gave the highly paid face workers the opportunity to buy into what had been hitherto the middle-class property market, instilled in the miners a robust confidence and at times a reckless independence in the 1970s and early 80s: their chests, said NUM president, Joe Gormley, were a mile wide. That the miners were so ebullient gave the nation the impression they were invincible, with the result that influential elements in the Conservative Party, convinced that the National Coal Board was a mere extension of the powerful union, decided to do something about Arthur Scargill, the class warrior, and what they regarded as a cock-eyed industry which continued to produce more and more coal — even when there was no demand.

Published in *The Economist* magazine in 1978, a Conservative Party document — the Ridley Plan — outlined radical proposals to combat big strikes. Almost unnoticed at the time of publication the plans played a crucial role in the 1984/85 miners' strike, one of the most divisive and bitter in the history of trade unions. In essence the plan mobilised the power of the state and public opinion against the union. At the same time the party looked at ways of dismantling the industry, reversing the tide of nationalisation.

The long road to the '84 strike began back in 1965 when the Yorkshire miners' council, shocked by the then closure programme, passed a resolution claiming that the Government's planning under their White Paper could not justify closing pits on uneconomic grounds alone. "This Council Meeting, speaking for Yorkshire, is of the opinion that, whilst there may be little we can do to oppose closures on the grounds of exhaustion, can and does strenuously oppose closures for solely uneconomic grounds." That was the first crack in the miners' hitherto rock solid support for the Labour Party, then in power. The resolution also signified that the Yorkshire miners, after years of single pit strikes, were beginning to harden their policies and widen their horizons. The 1960s was a period of great change and

anxiety, not least for the mining industry. Mechanization had brought great leaps in productivity but the pits in Scotland, Durham and parts of Yorkshire were getting older and were closing at a faster rate than in the past. As early as November, 1961, Mr. Roy Mason, MP for Barnsley, said the NCB had the wrong image. "It is time

Below: Arthur Scargill, president of the Yorkshire miners, in the early 1980s.

the Minister (of Power) tried to create a fresh image in the minds of the miners instead of the existing one — that of an octopus extending its tentacles throughout the coalfields and squeezing them to death." The Plan for Coal envisaged the closure of 200 pits over the next five years, although the Tory Minister of Power, Mr. R. Wood, said pits would close but output and the number of mineworkers would rise by 1965. On top of closures there was fierce competition from "modern" fuels such as cheap oil and nuclear power. When 70,000 Yorkshire miners came out on strike over surface men's hours in 1969, Jack Leigh, the Yorkshire vice president, put it all in a nutshell: "Everybody in the coalfield knows that coal is fighting for its existence and the Yorkshire miners have reached the end of the road." Councillor Bill O'Brien, secretary of the North Yorkshire Panel of the NUM (and now MP for Normanton), commenting on coal board threats to close Park Mill Colliery during the strike, said: "We have lived so long as mice that the coal board will still close pits, strike or not." The unofficial strike, which involved other coalfields, was a watershed. Left wing miners had almost forgotten what it was like to organise a widespread strike. Involving 130,000 miners and 140 pits, the strike, like the

1893 and 1912 disputes, demonstrated what mass action could do. It was also significant because it started in Yorkshire with the so-called "flying pickets," the precursors of the famous pickets in the 1970s.

Miners, who had been at the top of the wages league after the war and who were still highly paid in 1958, were twelfth in 1970. Their deteriorating position in the league led to another strike. The majority in the strike ballot on pay was not large enough to warrant an official strike under union rules and the subsequent unofficial strike was patchy and disorganised. Lord Robens, chairman of the NCB, claimed irresponsible militants were breaking all the rules and agreements because they did not like the final offer. At Doncaster he was met by "a yarling mob" of miners, Robens later believing that the mob was the new and unacceptable face of the union and that a new breed had been spawned, union bully boys. The strike demonstrated that the old relationship between the NCB and NUM was crumbling, that a change in the union rules on strike ballots was on the cards and that a new generation of young militants was flexing its muscles. In that year a number of rising union officials, including Arthur Scargill and Ron Rigby of Barnsley produced a pamphlet, "Miners:

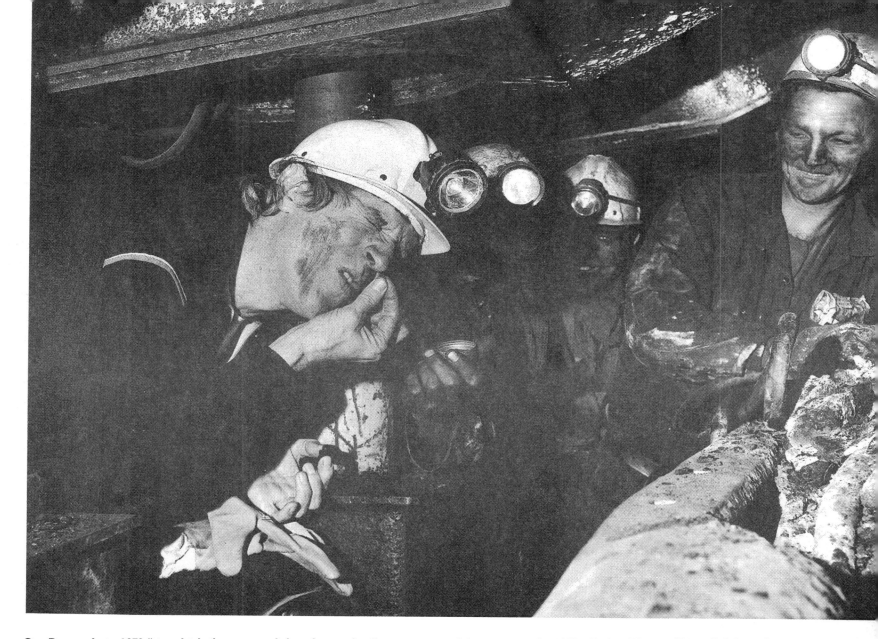

Above: D.J. Jimmy Saville, an ex-miner, taking snuff at South Kirkby Colliery, pre 1980.
B.J. Norton/British Coal.

Our Demands in 1970," in which they warned that the nation could not depend on cheap oil from the Middle East in the 70s and that coal was crucial to the future energy needs of the nation. Demanding change in the coal industry through action, they wrote: "As miners we were becoming disillusioned by the contraction of the industry. We started to seek individual solutions. Many of us left the industry. Absentee rates were high. We lost faith in our national leadership. Conciliation, negotiation, compromise brought no real gains. The unofficial strike last October (on surface men's hours) changed all that. The strike forced the NCB to grant its biggest wage increase ever. It rejuvenated the miners. It raised morale." Men like Scargill, then pit branch officials, started their rise to power at a time when the miners who had started work in the early 1920s, who were in general moderates, solid Labour Party supporters and anti-Communist were retiring and the number of working men who had working experience of the hungry decades was diminishing. The new miners had not known poverty, victimisation at work and the 1926 lock-out and had, therefore, no hang ups about taking on a Government – perhaps even a Labour Government.

Having achieved some success on the strike front the NUM activists were set for the big strikes which rattled the Government and the nation in the 1970s. At the NUM conference in 1971 the delegates approved a resolution which, the union said, would give them a decent living. At the same time the conference changed the rules to make strikes easier, a sign that the rising tide of militancy was having an impact. Mr Scargill said later: "After the 1969 and 1970 disputes it was clear that things would not be the same again. The pressures on the right wing were so intense that they realised that if they did not do something about the rules of the union, the left and the rank and file would sweep them aside. So they changed the rules of the union to allow strike action to be called with a fifty-five per cent majority instead of the two thirds majority. This was the most decisive rule change in the history of the union. In 1971 we were able to mobilise in every coalfield; we wanted a vote for action and we got it. We had a fifty-seven per cent vote nationally."

After the board had rejected a pay claim a special delegates' conference implemented a ballot on strike action and started an overtime ban. Starting in January, 1972, the strike had immediate success with the now famous flying pickets playing a crucial role, descending on pits, power stations and coal and coke depots. On Friday, January 7, the "Daily Express" declared: "A colliery shutdown will mean the death-warrant for more

Above and Right: The Barnsley coalfield was given a new look in the 1980s. Grimethorpe (above), Redbrook (right) and Houghton Main (extreme right).
British Coal.

of the nation's uneconomic pits. The major victims of the strike will be the miners themselves." The response was the proverbial burp from the bottom of the pit shaft. At that time newspapers and the public had not been programmed to accept that miners were capable of crippling the nation, just as in early 1984 the miners had not been programmed to accept the concept of defeat. The important events in 1972 were the body blows to industry: power black outs, the lay offs and the famous Battle of Saltley coking depot in Birmingham where pickets with massive support from other trade unions closed the gates, a turning point in the strike. The events demonstrated that miners were capable of bringing the nation to its knees. To the Conservative Party the closure of the gates was due to ineffective Policing and the pickets' role in the battle was seen as a victory for bully boys. Such views shaped the policies of the future Conservative Government via the Ridley plan. Meanwhile, the Court of Inquiry headed by Lord Wilberforce said the miners had an exceptional case and recommended a twenty-seven per cent wage rise.

Arthur Scargill, who took a leading role in the Saltley incident, was becoming a national figure, vilified by the right and loved by the young militants. Flowing with the left wing tide in the coalfield he was elected the union's Yorkshire compensation agent and then president, filling the vacuum left by the retirement of the elderly moderate leadership. He represented a new type of leader: brash, assertive and articulate with a taste for big cars and executive style suits. He had a reputation as a man who refused to compromise, promting one NCB official to declare: "Scargill did not negotiate – he just wore you down."

At their 1973 conference the national union prepared a wage claim of £35 a week for surface workers, £40 for underground workers and £45 for face workers. When the board rejected the claim in February, 1974, the miners voted eighty-one per cent in favour of strike action. Prime Minister Mr Edward Heath called a general election to try to obtain a vote of confidence from the electorate but the Labour Party won the election, after which they gave in to the miners.

With the dramatic rise in the price of Middle East oil – miners had been warning for years that Arabs would not want to live in tents all their lives – the new Labour Government decided that coal was the fuel of the future. Twenty years of decline in the industry were reversed and newspapers declared that King Coal was back on the throne. The Barnsley coalfield, badly hit by the closure programme in the 1960s, received a massive injection of £400 million aimed at concentrating production on three centres, Woolley, Grimethorpe and South Kirkby.

The nigger in the NUM woodpile came in 1978 with the publication of the Ridley Report, which recommended that a Conservative Government build up maximum coal stocks at power stations; make plans for importing more coal; encourage the recruitment of non-union lorry drivers by haulage contractors to enable the NCB to move coal; and introduce coal/oil firing facilities at all power stations as quickly as possible. Mr Nicholas Ridley believed the greatest deterrent to any strike would be "to cut off the money supply to the strikers and make the union finance them." On top of that he recommended the formation of a large mobile police force to uphold the laws against illegal picketing.

By the time the Thatcher Government was elected in May, 1979, politicans on the right were worried about both the NUM and the NCB, which they saw as an extension of the union. To anyone born within spitting

Above: The coal face.
British Coal.

Right: South Kirkby management team: Left to right back row: W. Bywater, B. Simpson, D. Thompson, A. Hirst, J. Henderson, J. Sumnall, B. Beverley.

Left: Barnsley seam, South Kirkby, showing the face entry, 1985.
J.B. Norton/British Coal.

distance of a coal mine, that seems to be an extraordinary view. The consensus in the pit communities had always been that the board, while an improvement on the old coal owners, were not angels and sometimes acted like a benevolent dictatorship. When the Government were considering a successor to Sir Derek Ezra as chairman, Roy Mason was on their possible list. Describing him as a "tough Labour moderate who understood Scargill," Nigel Lawson in his autobiography said Mason would not be disposed to "contract out the running of the industry to the NUM or give the unions a veto over national policy." Mr. Mason, now Lord Mason, has confirmed that Lawson submitted his name as a possible successor to Sir Derek, adding: "I did not get it from the horse's mouth but I gather I was turned down because Mrs Thatcher said: 'He is not one of us.' " Perhaps that was a sign the

Government were already looking for a blue-tinted axe man, rather than another Lord Robens; although he was an able man Robens was still, in the view of the Conservatives, an ex-Labour MP. Former NCB men would disagree with Lawson on the alleged subordinate role the NCB played in the industry, but there was a grain of truth in his views, since the union seemed to have an extraordinary amount of power and influence in the 1970s and early 1980s. Or an illusion of power.

On the NUM side some leaders were convinced that a confrontation was inevitable from May, 1979. In his annual report for 1980, Mr Owen Briscoe, Yorkshire miners' general secretary, wrote: "I, along with many others, am of the opinion that it is the intention of the Tory Government to decimate the coal industry," pointing out that Mrs Thatcher had agreed at a summit meeting on energy in Venice to expand the coal industry

117

Above: Mock face showing double ended ranging drum shearer, South Kirkby, 1985.
J.B. Norton

Right: Servicing the shearer Barnsley seam, South Kirkby, 1985.
J.B. Norton

yet a few weeks later had ordered two nuclear stations. "If that is not the height of hypocrisy, and a pointer to pit closures, then the moon is made of green cheese," he wrote. But that was it: no more words on pit closures. The rest of the report dealt with bathing and changing time payments (that was probably the most significant argument between the board and the union's Yorkshire area that year), the exploitation of black labour in South Africa and the danger of nuclear confrontation between the major powers, an indication that pit closures had not become a burning issue at that time, although Scargill, still Yorkshire president, was making threatening noises on projected pit closures. The situation changed rapidly. In 1981 Yorkshire miners gave their leaders permission to call a strike in the event of pit closures and the resolution was put in a filing cabinet to await the confrontation. Then Mr Ian MacGregor, aged seventy, and chairman of the Amax Corporation in the USA which had substantial coal mining interests, was appointed chairman of the NCB in 1983: a tough Scots American businessman chosen to reorganise the industry on business lines and to take on the NUM, particularly Scargill. By 1983 the industry was in turmoil. Management were taking a tougher line and miners, afraid their jobs were in jeopardy, became belligerent.

In his annual report presented in March, 1983, Jack Taylor, the Yorkshire miners' President, said:" I believe

Above: South Kirkby Colliery miners who achieved a European productivity record, 1981. *British Coal*

Left: Shearer cutting coal, Newhill seam, South Kirkby. *J.B. Norton*

Far Left: Advancing powered supports, Newhill seam, South Kirkby, 1985. *J.B. Norton*

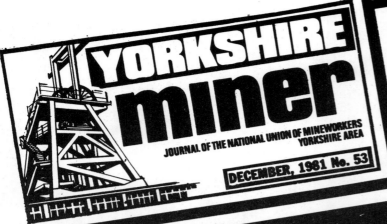

YORKSHIRE miner

JOURNAL OF THE NATIONAL UNION OF MINEWORKERS YORKSHIRE AREA

DECEMBER, 1981 No. 53

SEE PAGES SIX, SEVEN AND EIGHT

SCARGILL FOR PRESIDENT

By OWEN BRISCOE, Yorkshire NUM General Secretary

We can speak and write all the fancy words in the world, but at the end of the day this election comes down to one thing: The type of person YOU are.

You either elect a leader who is prepared to stand up and be counted on the major issues — job security, pay, hours, protection of earnings, pensions, health, safety and the like — or you take another path.

That path can best be described in two words: British Leyland.

There we witnessed the pitiful sight of a workforce kicked in the teeth by the very boots it has been forced to lick over recent years.

PAYMASTERS

Such a path can never be trodden by miners. We come from a proud and dignified tradition, but over the years so much of our energy has had to be spent battling on two fronts: With the Coal Board and with the National Leadership of our own union.

Now, however, at long last we have it in our power to elect a leader who will fight tooth and nail for the men he is privileged to represent.

Without question, such a man is Arthur Scargill.

The things which Arthur has said over the years might not have been to the liking of certain people, but that's not what it's about; the man who never upset anyone, the man who just limited himself to saying what others wanted to hear, cannot be true to anybody, including himself.

Making sure that your pit stays open so that you and your sons can have work; putting more money into your pocket; or fighting for any of the other issues which are so important *is* a tough business, but that's what you pay your union dues for.

You are the paymasters and you are entitled to expect the best service possible from the NUM, not just at pay claim time, but every day of the year, handling all the bread and butter issues which never hit the headlines.

I've seen what Arthur Scargill has done in Yorkshire and I know how much he could achieve for the members as national President.

And that's why I want to add just one more thing: Give him the biggest percentage majority ever recorded for a national trade union leader.

That would give us a marvellous head start in future negotiations with the Coal Board.

For they would be left in no doubt whatever that Arthur Scargill speaks for Britain's mineworkers.

Vote Scargill on December 2nd, 3rd and 4th and at long last give us a leadership which puts the members first.

As for the other candidates, I'll just limit myself to one comment: These three Stooges could do for the NUM what a short back and sides did for Samson.

Right: The Conservative government came to the conclusion that a national strike was inevitable when Arthur Scargill was elected president.

Opposite Right: 1983 when a miners' demonstration (in Barnsley) reflected the power of the union. By 1987 the union was a shadow of its former self.
Don Oakes.

122

that very shortly this union will be put to the test in determining the future size and shape of the coal industry. Also at stake is the self-respect and credibility of the union. The future is in our hands." The penultimate sentence is illuminating. Although the impending strike was chiefly over pit closures, there was also another element, the reputation the all-powerful miners had among their fellow trade unionists: the miners' leaders felt it was their responsibility to ram-raid the Government on behalf of others. When leaders like Taylor talked of "credibility" and "self respect" — and Scargill talked of bringing down the Government — the Conservatives took note and muttered about the enemy within. In his report, Mr. Taylor also pointed out that the NCB had grown in confidence following the recent union leaders' defeat in the national ballot on wages and pit closures (in favour of industrial action: 39 per cent nationwide, 56 per cent in Yorkshire): "Their attitude at all levels of management has become less understanding and more intransigent. We now find ourselves confronted with a take it or leave it attitude."

A strike that year at Dodworth Colliery was a sign of things to come in what had become a fractious industry. A relatively minor incident — a miner was sacked for allegedly striking a deputy — exploded like a powder keg. Dodworth sent pickets to all the Barnsley pits and, with miners refusing to cross picket lines, the Barnsley coalfield was at a standstill for a time; at the NCB's Barnsley area headquarters at Grimethorpe there were rumblings that union militants were stirring up trouble, trying to turn the Dodworth dispute into a major coalfield confrontation between employer and employees. However, Dodworth was more likely to have been a spontaneous outburst of pent up anger, a strike right from the gut of the rank and file with no one pulling strings. After all, deputies were more hated than pit managers and the miners demanded the reinstatement of their mate, described by the men as a gentle giant. Bloody-minded and stubborn the Dodworth miners — who had a reputation for militancy — even clashed with their union branch delegate and area union leaders who recommended a return to work pending negotiations on the sacking; the leaders, including Jack Taylor, got it in the neck when they were heckled and booed at a belligerent mass meeting at Dodworth towards the end of the dispute. The reporters who attended that meeting said they could detect an explosive mixture in the air that day, an atmosphere they would feel again on the violent picket lines during the course of the year long strike. The Dodworth strike demonstrated that the old order in the industry, since the mid 1970s a cosy relationship between the lower ranks of the union and the NCB — some pit personnel officers and manpower officers at area level were former moderate NUM branch officials — was breaking down and chaos was spreading. It also revealed there was a prodigious amount of raw energy and anger just waiting to be released. Miners at Dodworth were not only ready to picket other pits — and Doncaster collieries, it was rumoured — they were prepared to confront and insult their own leaders. To the outsider it appeared as if no one was in charge of the rattling coal trains marked NUM and NCB.

Right: Yorkshire miners' demonstration in Barnsley, 1983.

In the run-up to the year long strike, during the NUM ban on overtime, similar pit strikes broke out all over the South Yorkshire coalfield, many of which were over petty issues. In contrast to the Dodworth strike it now seemed as if someone in the NCB or NUM was continually pushing a button marked "strike." Industrial relations having hit a new low, the union's Barnsley Miners' Panel were about to discuss the strikes when the NCB dropped a bombshell by announcing the closure of Cortonwood and Bullcliffe Wood in March, 1984, an illogical decision if the board wanted better industrial relations, since the closure of a pit with substantial reserves – Cortonwood – was bound to antagonise the union. It is already part of Labour mythology that the miners were set up for a strike, that Cortonwood, a moderate pit in the centre of the union's Yorkshire heartland, was selected for closure in order to bump-start the overtime ban into a strike. However, according to the then NCB Director for South Yorkshire, George Hayes, he had been asked to reduce capacity and Cortonwood was the obvious choice, the board having failed to sell Cortonwood coal which was piling up at the pithead. By closing Cortonwood at that time he could more or less guarantee miners jobs at other pits. Now it has been suggested in Paul Routledge's "Scargill" that the plan to strike in March may have been prepared months in advance by the NUM, not the NCB, and the journalist refers to a conversation between Jimmy Cowan, deputy chairman of NCB, and Mick McGahey, the NUM vice president, in which McGahey is alleged to have spilled the beans, saying the strike would start in March in Yorkshire. Later McGahey said he had been talking in general terms. Had March been fixed in advance as the date of the strike – and Cortonwood had not closed – what would the NUM have used as fuse paper? A pit had to close before a strike could be called. Much has been written about so-called conspiracy theories, mainly from the left wing who claim the state in cohorts with the NCB and Fleet Street engineered the strike and then ganged-up with the judiciary to nobble the miners. But perhaps there was no conspiracy on either side –just a cock-up!

On the day the closure was announced it took sometime before television grasped what was happening. The closure item was the third or fourth item on the evening regional television news programme that Friday night, a blatant error, for someone in the news room had not realised the significance of the event or perhaps the item had arrived too late for it to be given the appropriate treatment. For the subsequent year the strike was never off the television screens.

The significance of the closure was not lost on the miners. The 1981 resolution was removed from the filing cabinet and the strike began three days after the closure announcement by the National Coal Board, 55,000 Yorkshire miners stopping work. What followed was a year dominated by violence, hard poverty and searching questions on a series of issues, including the state of

Below: Dodworth Colliery, scene of a pit strike in 1983.

THE MINER

Journal of the National Union of Mineworkers   October, 1982

DAILY BLAH

SIDALL SAYS
- 30/50,000 JOBS TO GO
- ONLY 7.2% ON PAY
- NO 4 DAY WEEK
- NO EARLY RETIREMENT
- NO ALLOWANCE CHANGES
- NO RATE PROTECTION

"After that lot he should change his name to sod-all!"

THE CRUNCH

BY NUM PRESIDENT ARTHUR SCARGILL

No playing with words; no messing about.

This is the most important NUM ballot in your life.

What you do will decide the future of Britain's coal industry.

Either we bow the knee and accept closures and a cut in living standards; or we fight like men, giving heart to the whole of our country.

For be under no illusions what this ballot is about.

Miners are the last major barrier to the continued wholesale slaughter of jobs and industries.

Over the last 16 months alone, 22,000 pit jobs have gone by stealth.

Now they are looking for the slightest sign of weakness so that the mad dogs of pit butchery can be fully unleashed. That's why pits like Snowdon, Kinneil and Britannia, with millions of tonnes in reserves, are already in their sights.

And pay isn't separate from all this. The Coal Board *itself* linked the two issues when they talked about "unit costs."

The message was unmistakeable. There might be more cash if we let some pits go to the wall.

BUT WE ARE NOT IN THE BUSINESS OF SELLING JOBS FOR PAY INCREASES.

And there's another way, too, in which both issues are entwined.

Every time the Board gets miners to accept a low pay rise, it says to itself that fear of unemployment is working.

So that actually *encourages* them to cut more jobs next year, keeping the fear going so that once again a small rise will be accepted.

But there comes a time, as with everything in life, when people have to say "enough's enough."

That time is now.

Over 60 years ago we were promised the four-day week. What have they said this time: Nothing doing.

Eaten away

Retirement at 55 for all mineworkers — something which other countries have had for decades — we're still battling for. And, yes, it is a scandal that a man who retires early gets just a few hundred pounds while a redundant mineworker gets thousands.

We've asked for equal treatment for the early retirers and the Board has just laughed in our face.

Our allowances have been eaten away by inflation and men through age or sickness have had to transfer to lighter jobs have seen pay rates slashed.

And as for pay itself, there's £812m which could be used for our 26 per cent claim — money which has come from a range of sources, including increased productivity and *our* job losses.

Right: The stage is set for 1984. "The Miner" newspaper states its case in 1982.

Opposite Right: Arthur Scargill during the strike.

MASS RALLIES

Hear OUR case from OUR leaders. President Arthur Scargill, General Secretary Lawrence Daly, Vice-President Mick McGahey and the full National Executive Committee will be there.

Monday, October 18th, 6.30 p.m., at the Afan Lido, Aberavon, Port Talbot (for the South Wales Area, Cokemen and COSA).

Tuesday, October 19th, 6.30 p.m., at the Digbeth Civic Hall, Birmingham (for the Midlands, South Derbyshire, Leicestershire, North Wales, COSA and Power Group areas).

Wednesday, October 20th, 6.30 p.m., at the City Hall, Northumberland Road, Newcastle on Tyne (for the Northumberland, Durham, Cokemen, Power Group, Group 1 and COSA areas).

Thursday, October 21st, 6.30 p.m., at the City Hall, Sheffield (for Yorkshire, Notts., North West, North Derbyshire, Cokemen, and Power Group areas).

Saturday, October 23rd, 11 a.m. at the Caley Cinema, Edinburgh (for the Scottish, Group 2, COSA and Cumberland areas).

THESE RALLIES ARE ABSOLUTELY VITAL TO **YOUR** FUTURE

DO ALL IN YOUR POWER TO BE THERE!

the coal industry, liberty, the power of the state, violence on both sides of the picket lines and the right of men to work during a strike. To digest the ramifications and present a balanced view of the strike is difficult even ten years on, so the strike has been condensed into this timetable: On March 8 the NUM executive gave official backing to the Yorkshire and Scottish strikes. By March 13 100,000 out of 180,000 were on strike in more than 90 of the country's 174 pits. Meanwhile the board announced a four million ton cut-back plan. On March 16 the Nottinghamshire miners voted not to strike and on April 12 Scargill ruled out a strike ballot. Towards the end of March the Central Electricity Generating Board claimed that power station coal stocks were at a record level for the time of the year. In mid-April former NUM delegate at Houghton Main, Terry Patchett, now MP for Barnsley East, claimed Police had been bugging miners' phones. Hoax information sent out by miners on the phone resulted in Police turning up at a meeting place, he said.

It became a violent strike with miners picketing pits in Nottinghamshire, rioting at Maltby Police Station in

Above: Cortonwood Colliery, 1984.
Stan Bulmer.

Below: Cortonwood miners march to Brighton in September, 1984, to lobby the TUC.

Above: Confrontation
between miners and police
outside the Yorkshire NUM
offices, Barnsley, March
1984.

June and clashing with police at Orgreave the same
month (ninety-three were arrested, seventy-nine
injured). Peace talks collapsed in July. On July 6, in the
Barnsley Chronicle, the NCB strongly refuted claims
that thousands of Barnsley pit jobs were at risk and
that local pits were in serious decline. A spokesman for
the board said: "Our plans are to maintain a stable
work force of between 12,500 and 13,000 mineworkers
for many years to come." And on August 1 Nigel Lawson
said the cost of the strike was a worthwhile investment
for the country and it was essential that the Government
spent whatever was necessary to defeat Scargill. In
September there were on-off talks and on the 20 th
Derbyshire miners won "a right to work" injunction.
There were more violent clashes at Maltby on September
24 when police appeared in boiler suits, and the Scottish
courts declared the strike in their areas official and
lawful. By October, at the Conservative Party
conference, John Gummer and Leon Brittan were

warning of a fight to the end against the miners.
November 12 saw the worst violence in Yorkshire when
petrol bombs were discovered. More men were going
back to work and the NCB claimed there were 1,900 "new
faces" on that day. At the Lord Mayor's banquet in
London Mrs Thatcher linked pickets with IRA bombers.
On December 17 MacGregor dashed the TUC peace
talks and John Paul Getty donated £120,000 to relieve
the distress of the miners. February 25 was a critical
date when 3,800 abandoned the strike, a high figure,
and the Welsh strike cracked for the first time. At a
special delegates conference at Congress House in
London ninety-eight voted for a return to work on March
3; ninety-one were against. The strike was over.

The strike in 1974 had made Scargill's reputation, the
strike of 1984/85 broke his power and the back of his
beloved union. Ten years after it started, the strike is
still debated, the causes and effects still mulled over.
The former aide to Arthur Scargill, Roger Windsor, now

a discredited figure in the ranks of the NUM, wrote later: "Let's face it, the NUM were never more than a bunch of amateurs trying to take on the might of the state. We lacked the cohesion, discipline and organisation to run any meaningful campaign, and were led by our Napoleon on to our battlefield at Waterloo." Windsor, hired as finance officer of the NUM in 1982, was later accused of being an MI5 agent by Labour MPs, a claim strenuously denied by Windsor. In the book, *The Coal Strike, Christian Reflections of the Miners' Struggle*, published in 1986, Brian Jenner wrote: "Few of the Yorkshire miners seriously doubted that the Tories deliberately chose conflict with the NUM. Two years previously it had been avoided, but now the loyalty of police and judiciary was assured after massive pay rises. The appointment of MacGregor to run the NCB was seen as a declaration of war and indeed the confrontational style in which he handled the dispute, and which has hardly abated since its end, brought dismay to many senior coal board officials." Dave Feickert, head of research at the NUM from 1983 to 1993, writing in *"The Guardian"* in October, 1993, stated: "If the strike was to be won as an industrial dispute, which it could have been, a deal would have had to be struck with the power unions early on. Indeed in May, 1984, Eric Hammond, the EEPTU electricians' leader, privately offered to ballot his power station members if the NUM would drop its political aims and ballot its own members. But Arthur found that politically unacceptable."

However, I believe that the strike failed because the NUM were still living in the 1970s, believing that old style picketing would win the day with some help from General Winter. But the Government, beginning with the Ridley Report, had prepared for a confrontation, just as the Baldwin Government had done in the 1920s in the run-up to the 1926 General Strike. In 1925 Baldwin

Above: Jack Taylor talks to a police officer after a miners demonstration in Huddersfield Road, March 1984.
R. Sabine

Below: Worsbrough pickets, victims of police reaction in Nottinghamshire, 1984.

had backed off on the grounds that other trade unions would support the miners. Between 1925 and 1926 they built up stocks of coal, imported coal and prepared a plan to keep essential supplies running in the event of a General Strike. When the miners were locked out, the TUC ordered a General Strike which soon fizzled out and the miners had to struggle on alone. The miners had made the mistake of depending too much on the goodwill of other trade unions. History repeated itself when the Conservative Government backed down over closures in 1981. David Howell, Mrs Thatcher's Energy Minister, appearing on televison in the latter stages of the 1984/85 strike, admitted that 1981 had not been the right time to take on miners. Coal stocks were relatively low and there was always a danger other trade unions would support the miners. By 1984, however, the trade unions were in retreat, the nation was sitting on mountains of coal and public opinion was against Scargill, who had become a figure of fun and the man-you-love-to-hate in the media.

Not everyone would agree that the Government and the NCB were the villains, since Arthur Scargill's election as President of the NUM was seen by the Government as a confrontational move, a throwback to the bad old days of the 1970s when the unions were said to have too much power; and he was elected with a staggering majority in 1982 — before MacGregor's appointment. In his autobiography, *The View from No. 11*, Lord Lawson said a strike was inevitable as soon as Scargill was elected, describing the NUM president as "a self-confessed, class-war revolutionary," a man "who spouted the most amazing nonsense" when they met soon after Scargill's election and whose decision to start the strike in spring was "astonishingly inept." Scargill not only disturbed the Government he frightened some of his own members. There was a great deal of pre-strike opposition to him in some of the coalfields, particularly Nottinghamshire, and I knew of some clandestine meetings involving pit winders from all over the country in Nottinghamshire long before the strike, meetings which had been called because of what they saw as Scargill's volatile and dangerous style of leadership. He was seen as a wrecker, a man who

Below: Mick Carter, NUM delegate at Cortonwood Colliery.

would destroy the union as well as the industry. The aim of the meetings: to test the water for a breakaway union of winders. Winders, who were in charge of the pit cages, always felt they were superior to miners and until about thirty years ago had their own union. The strike intervened and I heard no more about the meetings but within a few months the breakaway union, the Union of Democratic Miners, emerged in Nottinghamshire. Lord Lawson, in his autobiography, said the anti-Scargill attitude of the Midland miners helped them to win the strike, pointing out that a decision to persuade Michael Heseltine to consider the second application by the NCB to develop the Vale of Belvoir was used as a sweetener to the miners.

There was criticism about Scargill nearer home. As Brian Jenner wrote in *The Coal Strike* : "Contrary to some of the media images, support for the NUM leadership, as personified by Arthur Scargill, was by no means total and by no means uncritical, even in militant South Yorkshire. But if hard things were sometimes said against their own leaders, it was for Margaret Thatcher and Ian MacGregor that the real anger was reserved." Since the strike the pit closure programme has validated Scargill's predictions, according to his supporters; but when people say that he deserves credit because he had been right in his repeated predictions on projected closures, one of my friends, a former NUM branch official, replies: "That only proves that he was given confidential reports and that he can read."

In the opinion of many people Scargill is seen as the man who destroyed his union and the industry. But the strike would have occurred with or without Scargill. The Government were determined to make the industry pay its way — at any cost — and that meant pit closures on a large scale with large cuts in manpower. The miners would have had to stand and fight at some time; the history and the spirit of the union demanded it and perhaps that, in the end, was their most poignant weakness. That was as much the fault of the union, its philosophy and its structure as Scargill. It has been said that things would have been different under wily Joe Gormley, Scargill's predecessor, but Gormley was successful in the post 1975 period because he had a close working relationship with Sir Derek Ezra, the chairman of the NCB, and Ezra had gone by 1984, succeeded by men who would not compromise. Like Scargill, Gormley would have found himself in the same box canyon facing the new hard men in the NCB with the same shadowy figures lurking in the background. It is all hypothetical but what could Gormley have done but strike? Execute a strategic withdrawal from the canyon with the voices of young Cortonwood miners ringing in his ears: "You sold us down the river!" No miners' leader, moderate or militant, would have been prepared to do that. Scargill has also been criticised for prolonging the strike and putting his members through a winter of hardship. I am not sure whether Scargill could have pulled the plug on the strike — even if he had wanted to do so. As the Dodworth strike demonstrated in 1983, the union leaders are not always in control of events. In 1984 there was a hard-core of militants who were bitter-enders and whose slogan "We

Above: Ann Scargill, wife of the NUM president, at a soup kitchen during the miners' strike.
R. Sabine.

Opposite: Policemen chasing pickets at Woolley Colliery.
Stan Bulmer.

told Arthur no surrender" could be seen around the coalfield. Had Scargill surrendered, they would have crucified him, ripping apart the union. After Christmas, 1984, most of the pickets and activists realised it was all over but they wanted to soldier on until March to notch up the first anniversary.

To some extent I feel sorry for some pit managers and middle management in British Coal because they may have been conned. Whereas miners have always treated coal owners, the National Coal Board and the Government with justifiable scepticism, the white collar workers went along with the dismantling of the industry convinced that it would not go too deep but they, too, have found themselves without jobs. The Government assault on the industry was also an attack on the whole ethos of the NCB and its past. They were intent on breaking up the NCB as well as the union.

Nearly 50 years after nationalisation, the coal wheel has turned full circle. The Government, convinced that nationalisation is out of date, are privatising the mines, resurrecting what most people believed had been become an extinct species, coal owners. Today, June 25, 1993, an ad has appeared in *The Daily Telegraph* requesting tenders to buy Grimethorpe and Houghton, the last pits in the old Barnsley coalfield. Back in 1983 it was a different picture with the NCB predicting in *The Barnsley Chronicle* that all the Barnsley pits would make a £25 million profit in 1984/85, which turned out

131

to be the year of the strike. Was that true? Or was it part of a propaganda war to win the minds of the miners in the pre-strike period? As late as 1981 the NCB had described the coalfield re-construction as "one of the most extensive rejuvenation exercises in industrial history." Barnsley's 18 pits and 15,000 miners would move into the twenty-first century on "a secure and profitable footing." An article in *Barnsley, An Industrial Heritage*, published by Barnsley Chamber of Commerce added: "...by 1984 when we (NCB) start to reap the full benefits of our major schemes, Barnsley will be one of the most productive and profitable areas in the country." When the strike ended in 1985 the cut-backs started almost immediately, Barnsley pits losing 3,000 jobs within four months in the biggest shake-out of labour for more than twenty years, and a further 2,000 in 1986, dashing any hopes that the coalfield would make a profit, dashing hopes that the coalfield would survive into the twenty-first century. As well as pits, the area offices at Grimethorpe, which employed 500 workers, were closed and staff offered redundancy or transferred to new North Yorkshire headquarters at Allerton Bywater. Woolley Colliery, once one of the largest in Barnsley with more 2,000 on the books, closed in 1987, two years after North Gawber had been merged with Scargill's former pit. Then followed the closures of Redbrook, Riddings/Ferrymoor, Darfield Main, Royston, South Kirkby, Barnsley Main, the Denby Grange group of pits and finally Grimethorpe and Houghton Main.

The Barnsley coalfield had been one of the largest in the country and before the First World War the pits had exported to Russia, Germany and France: the high quality steam coal fuelled French warships as well as crack steam expresses in this country. In ten years the pits have been wiped out and more than £400 million investment (at 1980s values) has gone down the tube.

Below: Cortonwood.
D. Colborn.

Above and Left: The long road back: miners return to work at Grimethorpe (above) and Havercroft (left).

133

Above: The pit buzzer.

Right: The fitters' shop.

Below: The pit yard.
Cortonwood Colliery, 1984, D. Colborn.

134

Above and Left:
Cortonwood before
closure.
D. Colborn.

Left: Demolition at
Cortonwood.
Stan Bulmer

135

Right: Maurice Peaker
(manager) and Paul Lewis
(deputy manager), South
Kirkby (Newhill seam),
1985.
J.B. Norton/British Coal.

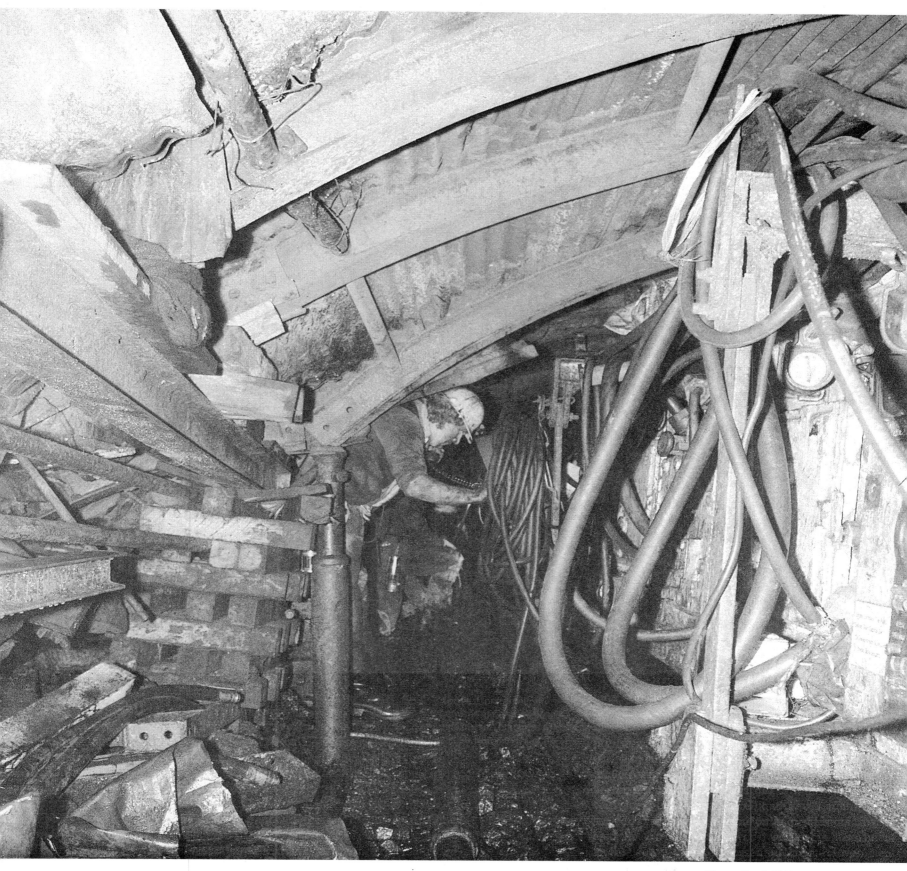

Above: South Kirkby, 1985/86. Advancing long wall face. 20m from the face entry, showing severe convergence.
J.B. Norton.

Above: North Gawber Colliery, merged with Woolley in 1985.

Right: Darfield Main Collliery, "closed" in 1985, then reprieved and later merged with Houghton.

Chapter 6
The October Revolution

"It is an extraordinary Government that can make Arthur Scargill a hero," said Patrick Hannan on a news programme, *Tea Junction* on BBC Radio 4 in April, 1993. Probably the most hated man in this country in the 1970s and 1980s Arthur led a march for jobs through some of London's wealthiest areas in October, 1992, and was mobbed by admirers. The same people who had jeered at miners and shaken fists at the television screens during the 1984/85 miners' strike were now applauding the miners because the Government had become more unpopular than miners, and that takes some achieving! "He was the man they loved to hate," trumpeted the *Daily Mirror* the following day. "But yesterday, thanks to bungling John Major, Arthur Scargill was both a hero to rich and poor. In swanky Park Lane, an admirer handed Arthur a bouquet of white chrysanthemums — and even the Police shared in Arthur's delight." The whole nation seemed to be behind Arthur and the miners after the Government had announced the big pit closure programme in October: thirty-one pits and 30,000 job losses. For the first time in more than fifty years miners were receiving widespread public support and Arthur, vilified by the tabloids for decades, chimed with the times. These were indeed extraordinary times. President of the Board of Trade, Mr. Michael Heseltine, was castigated for his handling of the closures — small when compared to the scale of the closures in the 1960s, during which one out of every two jobs in the industry vanished, and to the 70,000 job losses announced by British Telecom over the last three years — and there was a backbench revolt by Tory MPs led by Winston Churchill, grandson of the man the miners loved to hate: a figure who was despised by two generations of miners. Scargill and a Churchill on the same side? Strange bedfellows indeed; Arthur's late father, a miner who lived through that appalling decade, the 1920s, would have been nonplussed. Tory MP Michael Clark admitted: "The Government has misread the mood of the country and the mood of the miners. They do not want charity."

The groundswell of public indignation against the proposed closures was not just motivated by a sense of injustice or love of miners; there had been a growing cynicism about the new Government since its election

Below: In August 1992, the statue on the Oaks Disaster Monument at Kendray had to be removed for repairs. The monument had stood since 1913. In October 1992, the closure of the last Barnsley pits was announced...

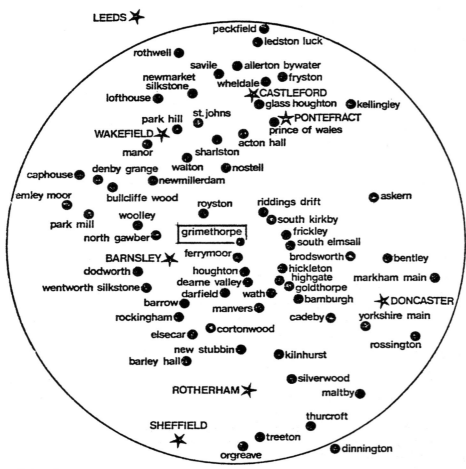

LEEDS ✴
peckfield
rothwell
ledston luck
savile
allerton bywater
newmarket
silkstone
wheldale
fryston
lofthouse
CASTLEFORD ✴
glass houghton
kellingley
park hill
st. johns
WAKEFIELD ✴
PONTEFRACT ✴
prince of wales
manor
sharlston
acton hall
denby grange
walton
nostell
caphouse
newmillerdam
emley moor
bullcliffe wood
royston
riddings drift
askern
woolley
south kirkby
park mill
grimethorpe
frickley
north gawber
south elmsall
BARNSLEY ✴
ferrymoor
brodsworth
bentley
dodworth
houghton
hickleton
highgate
markham main
wentworth silkstone
dearne valley
goldthorpe
darfield
wath
barrow
barnburgh
DONCASTER ✴
rockingham
manvers
cadeby
yorkshire main
elsecar
cortonwood
new stubbin
rossington
barley hall
kilnhurst
silverwood
ROTHERHAM ✴
maltby
thurcroft
SHEFFIELD ✴
treeton
dinnington
orgreave

Below: The modern washery at Woolley.
Don Oaks, Barnsley Chronicle.

in April, 1992, and the closures proved to be a catalyst. (A similar mood, cynical and corrosive, had been detected in America where big government was under attack from public opinion, a mood which led to the election of an outsider, Bill Clinton, as President in November, 1992). It is difficult to get excited when the Government is booted out of the Exchange Rate Mechanism or euphoric when discussing the finer points of the Maastricht treaty, but "blood on coal" is an emotive and straightforward subject, the massaging of which enables a nation to let off frustration and steam. Later, with rising unemployment and further gaffes by the Government, the sting went out of public protests on pit closures and when the pits closed there was hardly a whisper of protest from the general public. The popularity of the Government continued to slide and by May, 1993, it was said to be the most unpopular since the war, Gallup revealing that the Government's approval rating had fallen to sixteen per cent. Only the first Wilson administration in 1968 had rivalled Major's lack of public esteem, with a figure of eighteen per cent. Large majorities of voters — more than sixty per cent — thought Major's Government was ineffective, short-sighted and out of touch.

But that was cold comfort in May in the Labour stronghold of Barnsley, where the remnants of the old coalfield, Houghton Main and Grimethorpe, closed. Despite a big campaign and big parades to try to keep the pits open, Houghton shut on the last day in April, Grimethorpe a week later. The men at Grimethorpe

Look after their future...

Opposite Top: The Yorkshire coalfield in 1978.

Left: A fact sheet produced by the Coalfield Communities group.

Britain is often called an island of coal. Reserves are measured in hundreds of years. If the mines close much of this will be lost for ever.

Britain has limited alternative energy sources. Nuclear power is too expensive (at least 3 times more than coal) and requires substantial ~~gov~~ernment subsidy. Gas reserves are scarce – only 40 ~~yea~~rs at the present rate of consumption, far less if ~~us~~ed to generate electricity.

Most experts say electricity from gas is more expensive than that from coal, even if coal power stations are fitted with equipment needed to burn coal cleanly.

If our coal mines are closed, Britain will become reliant on imported coal and gas for its electricity. A recent government report admits that over 80% of our energy needs will be imported by the year 2000.

Most British pits are now profitable and production costs are still tumbling. Experts (including the power generators) predict that within five years British coal will be as cheap as imported coal – sooner if the exchange rate continues to fall.

British mines are the most efficient in Europe and receive no government subsidy. They produce coal 50% cheaper than in Germany and Spain. Both of these nations financially support their coal industry because they recognise the importance of having their own secure energy supplies.

In the last five years, the cost of Britain's coal has gone down 28% in real terms, but electricity prices have continued to rise. This indicates there is something seriously wrong with the electricity market. We know that one distortion is the £1.3 billion annual subsidy to nuclear power paid for by you, the consumer, in your electricity bill. But no-one will reveal how much extra consumers will pay to cover the higher costs of electricity from the new gas stations.

Elsewhere in the developed world, countries are moving massively away from nuclear and expensive oil towards coal for electricity production. The USA's use of coal is set to rise 20% in the 1990s.

In a time of deep recession and against a backcloth of flawed economic evidence, the government is to spend at least £2 billion to close pits – much of it on redundancy payments and unemployment benefits.

Last but by no means least is the unnecessary destruction of the livelihoods of 30,000 miners and at least as many again in supporting industries. They don't want aid, they want to keep working.

10 REASONS why the 31 threatened Coal Mines should stay open

141

agreed to take British Coal's enhanced redundancy package, the same package accepted earlier by the Houghton men. Grimethorpe NUM branch secretary Ken Hancock said: "There seems to be a cloud of despair hanging over the whole community. There is a smell of fear and uncertainty not only at the pit but in the village," a quote reminiscent of the one made by the young miner at Cortonwood Colliery when he appeared for a few seconds on News at Ten after the announcement to close the pit in 1984: "Unless we save this pit there is going to be a plague right up the (Dearne) Valley." Mr. Hancock was upset but not surprised that the 210 men made the two-to-one decision to accept the package.

The Grimethorpe closure marked the end of the 30 year decline in the Barnsley coalfield. In 1961 half the town's working population was engaged in mining and quarrying and the coalfield employed 33,500. But Barnsley Council were already warning that new industry was needed to replace old pits. By the mid 1960s the Government's first big pit closure programme was on the way and the axe fell on the Barnsley coalfield, one of the oldest in the country, and in six years the pits went down like ninepins: Haigh, Wharncliffe Silkstone, Monk Bretton, Wombwell Main, the Wharncliffe Woodmoor Collieries at Carlton, Barnsley Main and the Monckton collieries. There was no public outcry. Lord Mason, a former Labour Minister of Power and former MP for Barnsley, said in one year in the 1960s thirty pits closed nationwide. But at that time there

were still plenty of pits where redundant miners could find a job and the nation's unemployment levels were not high. He introduced the over fifty-five scheme which enabled redundant men who did not get a job to receive financial assistance until the age of sixty-five: "the real beginnings of miners' redundancy payments," said the former Barnsley miner. By 1974 the Barnsley coalfield employed nearly 20,000, half the 1960 figure. Saleable output had fallen from eleven million to below seven million tonnes in the same period. An NCB (Barnsley) official said in 1974: "Despite the age of the coalfield (the average age of the pits is over eighty years), the twenty-four seams now being worked contain 268 million tonnes of classified workable reserves, including 60 per cent of the national coking coal reserves." For a while

the coalfield seemed to be in terminal decline but then massive investment at local pits – following an unexpected upsurge in the demand for coal – resulted in the NCB in 1983 still being the most single economic influence on the borough and the biggest single employer, operating the following pits: Dodworth/Redbrook, North Gawber, Woolley, Grimethorpe, Houghton Main, Barrow/Barnsley Main (in the process of reopening), Ferrymoor/Riddings, Darfield Main, Kinsley Drift, Dearne Valley, South Kirkby, Royston Drift and the Denby Grange, Bullcliffe Wood group. The NCB paid two million pounds in wages into the local economy every week and a similar figure in rates to the local council. It was a smaller, rejuvenated coalfield, one of the most modern in the world; it had

Above: Arthur Scargill, a hero in 1992.

been created by pumping more than £400 million into the pits and cutting the number of workers. A report by Barnsley Council, Coal Mining and Barnsley, published in 1983, stated: "It has been Barnsley's good fortune to have good coal reserves, using the Government's criterion, to justify the investment it has received, while other areas now face the complete collapse of their coal industries. It is ironic that the shedding of over 20 per cent of the NCB's Barnsley area workforce in a decade can be classed as good fortune..." Between 1977 and 1983 5,750 out of nearly 20,000 Barnsley mining jobs were lost and, according to the report, management planned to shed at least 1,000 more by the end of 1985 "though no colliery is immediately at risk." It was anticipated that by 1986 there would be 16,000 mineworkers in Barnsley. The pre-strike shedding of labour in Barnsley pits was done with the approval of the unions as part of the modernisation programme, but there was an understanding that the remaining jobs would be retained for years. Had there not been the modernisation programme pits would have closed before the strike. The 1984/85 miners strike, triggered off by the closure of Cortonwood and Bullcliffe Wood Collieries, was a watershed in many respects, ushering in a new era in the industry. The NUM argued that the strike was planned and implemented by the NCB and

the Government to break the power of the union to pave the way for the dismantling of the nationalised industry. Within months of the end of the strike British Coal, formerly the National Coal Board, began carving up the Barnsley coalfield.

The first sign of the shape of things to come appeared when British Coal did not open Redbrook and Barnsley Main in a fanfare of publicity at the end of the strike in March, 1985. Dodworth and Barrow had been closed under the modernisation programme and a reduced workforce transferred to Redbrook, which had been rebuilt, and Barnsley Main, a new pit on the site of the old colliery closed in the 1960s. The strike interrupted the transfer of men and the official openings. Before the strike the new pits had assured futures; after the strike coal became a new ball game with new rules and a new referee and linesmen, and British Coal knew both mines would not survive many years in the new harsh climate, so the pits were opened without any fuss.

Other pits where millions of pounds had been invested and where jobs had been originally "guaranteed" for fifteen or twenty years were closed over the next few years because the pits could not match new productivity yardsticks. After the strike the economic goal posts were moved: pits had to produce more coal at a lower cost. On top of that each pit had to repay the high

Left: Grimethorpe miners at a protest meeting in October, 1992.

NOT DOLE
THE RIGHT TO WORK. FOR ALL OUR FUTURES

SACK MAJOR NOT THE MINERS

Above: Ian Walker, a Grimethorpe miner and son, Richard.

Right: The youthful face of coal mining — a Grimethorpe miner.
W. Hobson, Barnsley Chronicle.

Above and Below:
Protests at local and national level. The Barnsley Women against Pit Closures are seen in London during the October demonstration.

interest on its capital investment, instead of it coming out of a central or regional fund, and in the case of the Barnsley pits there had been hugh investment: more money than in any other coalfield apart from Selby. "We are being crippled by high interest charges," became a familiar quote from NUM branch officials as the pits closed. What had been seen as the saviour of the old Barnsley coalfield — investment — now became a cross that was too heavy to carry and between 1985 and 1993 pits were closed at a faster than anticipated rate. Meanwhile, questions were asked about the validity of the investment in the first place. Why was so much

money invested in an old coalfield where the seams were thin? How could a "new" coalfield disappear so fast? The NCB argued that the market for Barnsley coking coal, the coalfield's prize asset, had been scaled down over the years. The country's largest reserves of coking coal were under the 120 square mile coalfield but the market collapsed with the contraction of the old steel industry before the coalfield reconstruction programme was complete. It was also pointed out that a "new" coalfield took many years to plan and bring into full production, and during that period markets and the needs of the national economy — or, perhaps, the

energy fads of the two principal political parties – could change beyond recognition.

By October, 1992, only Grimethorpe and Houghton Main remained in the once mighty Barnsley coalfield, both pits having seen big reductions in manpower in the aftermath of the strike. Then they were included in the doomed list of thirty-one pits. Arthur Scargill, describing the October closure programme as vandalism, said: "The only reason for closing these pits is an act of vindictiveness on the part of the Tory Government and on the part of the people who want to destroy the NUM. It is nothing but malice for 1974."

(Scargill is consistent: in the 1960s he used emotive language about pit closures; in 1980 he claimed that the NCB had secret plans for the closure of up to fifty pits over three years, an allegation denied by the board at the time). What followed became known as the People's Revolt, with *"The Observer"* declaring on October 18: "John Major is facing a catastrophic Commons defeat over pit closures unless the Government makes substantial concessions." Tory MPs believed that public feeling was so strong that the Government might have to promise a review – and a delay – to the pit closure programme.

Above: A demonstration in Barnsley.

Right and Opposite Page: Miners and their wives and children protest at pit closures — pictured in London and en route to the capital by Barnsley Chronicle Photographers.

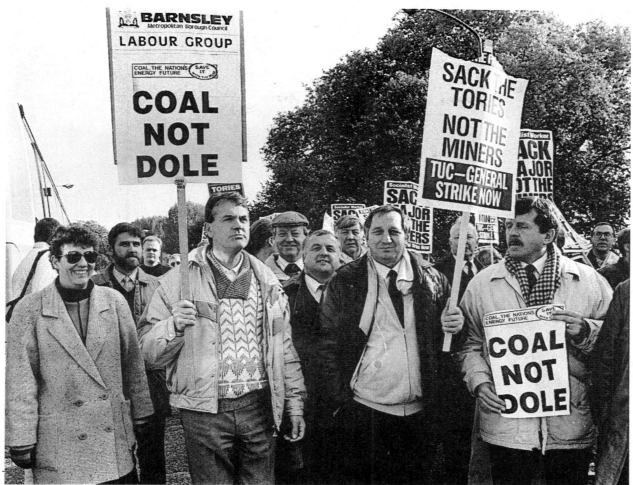

However, Neil Clarke, BC's chairman, told the Trade and Industry select committee that only a radical transformation of the market for coal would save the pits and at present there was no market for the coal. Miners had been breaking productivity records but the coal was piling up at the pitheads. British Coal officials argued that if the Government had split the power generators into four or five companies, the "dash for gas" would not have occurred, and the need for such massive colliery closures would have been avoided. By October 19, after a public outcry, Heseltine was forced into announcing a provisional reprieve for some pits and consultation on others. On March 26, however, the Barnsley Chronicle announced that Grimethorpe and Houghton had not been given a reprieve – but the fight went on – with Ken Hancock saying: "We have got to fight on or accept that for the rest of our lives we will be on the dole – I am not going to settle for that." NUM national vice president Frank Cave said: "Despite the public anger over this issue and despite all the evidence and arguments in favour of maintaining the UK coal industry, Michael Heseltine has announced the closure of thirty-one pits. The Government knows the market is rigged against coal. They know that electricity from gas and nuclear power is more expensive but they have chosen to do nothing about it." *The Observer* said: "The essential problem for the industry is that the Government is neither prepared to protect the market for coal nor devise a coherent long-term energy policy based on the balanced use of Britain's oil, coal, gas, nuclear and other resources...." "New or planned gas-fired power stations are scheduled to replace up to thirty million tonnes of coal by the late 1990s..." "Nuclear receives a subsidy of £1.2 billion a year, which if

149

Above: Hedley Salt, leader of Barnsley Council, speaking at a demo in Barnsley.

magically transferred to the pits would transform the economics of the mining industry." In June "The Observer" announced: "It was a swift, silent execution. Nineteen coal mines have closed in the past six weeks, pushing to 18,000 the number of miners made redundant since October. More casualties are expected by the end of the year. Yet hardly a placard has been waved in protest. Eight months after the nation rose up in anger at Michael Heseltine's plans to shut thirty-one pits, the

President of the Board of Trade is well on the way to achieving his original goal almost unchallenged. Only a handful of the reprieved mines are expected to survive. The miners are still protesting and demonstrating, but they are fighting a forgotten war. And they are weakened by deadlines for accepting redundancy."

Seumas Milne, in *The Guardian* wrote: "If ever there was a testament to the cynicism of public life in the 1990s, it must surely be the silent six-week closure of

Below: Ann Scargill (right) wife of the president of the NUM, pictured outside pit gates in Barnsley.

Above: A torchlight protest at Grimethorpe.
W. Hohson.

Left: The pit closure programme displayed in placards.

Top: Grimethorpe Colliery.

Below and Opposite Below: Farewell to Grimethorpe Colliery ceremony, May 14, 1993. A wreath was laid to commemorate the men who died at the pit.

almost half of the British coal industry. Since the end of April, nineteen pits have been shut and their work forces bullied and cajoled off colliery books. More than 17,000 miners have been made redundant since last October . . . 'all this has been executed without a murmur from either Government or opposition, media or trade unions. One miner said that if they blew up the pit now they (the media) would not report it. It was all so different last October." In Lord Lawson's words: "Diversification of energy sources . . . was code for freedom from NUM blackmail."

Heseltine was still saying there was no market for coal — and Labour politicans were still claiming that the energy markets had been "rigged" in favour of gas — when Grimethorpe-Houghton went up for sale as one unit in June as part of the coal privatisation programme. Meanwhile, across the old Barnsley coalfield, millions of tons of coal remain sterilised underground, the shafts are being filled in and on former pit sites like Cortonwood work is under way to produce new industry. At Redbrook, reopened in 1985 after a £20 million investment programme and closed a few years later, a bustling business park stands on the site: not even the Japanese move that fast. And at the former Dodworth pit a Japanese company, Koyo Seiko, a ball bearings manufacturer, is already in production. Whether such schemes will lift Barnsley out of the economic pit remains to be seen. Back in the nineteenth century mining saved the town from economic collapse when the linen industry declined. What will save Barnsley today?

Left: The farewell ceremony with father and daughter in tears. Note the message on the helmet: "Goodbye Grimey". *Press Association.*

Above: Grimethorpe 1993. *W. Hobson.*

Mining memories

At the age of twelve, in 1936, Roy Mason was at the pit-head at Wharncliffe Woodmoor 1/2/3 when the bodies were brought out: he remembered vividly the huddled groups of women in shawls and the weeping; Father King, who led thousands in prayer at the pit head; the temporary mortuary in the school hall near the pit; and George Formby appearing at a later fund-raising show at the Alhambra Cinema.

Two years later, on his second shift at the sister pit, Wharncliffe Woodmoor 4/5 he saw a dead man carried out on a stretcher. "My charge-hand said they always brought out dead men feet first with a cover over the body."

The future Labour minister was buried three times at the 4/5 colliery. On one occasion he was talking to two men in charge of a power machine when a shouted warning alerted him to danger. "Mr Laverack, who saved my life, shouted 'Look out!'. He had seen a prop buckle. I found myself spread-eagled with a large stone on my back. My lamp had gone out and it was dusty, but I could see lamps bobbing about in the distance and I shouted for help. I was carried out on a stretcher badly bruised."

Injuries were nothing new to the Mason family. His grandfather lost an eye and his father was crippled for life, dying at the age of 60. His father was a committed trade unionist and on his first pay day (wage 19s. 6d.) his father told him to go to the union office and pay his contributions. He has been a member of the union for 49 years.

Private enterprise was the arch enemy. The coal getters received a small basic wage and the bonus depended on the number of full tubs. Sometimes there was a shortage of empty tubs; delays caused frustration and when an empty tub appeared miners fought each other to claim ownership. The market system, whereby a group of men who did not have regular jobs were directed to fill vacancies elsewhere, gave deputies enormous power and influence. They could pick their mates for the best jobs, leaving the rest to be transferred to lower paid jobs.

The village had its own class system, Long Row being for the miners, Stone Row for the deputies and the large detached house for the manager.

The 1930s were hungry years with the demand for coal remaining depressed and pits closed for part of the week. Miners worked three days and had three days off, receiving three days pay and three days dole. If the pit opened for a fourth shift it was not uncommon for someone to sabotage a shift by removing a prop to cause a roof fall. Some of the men were then sent home. The miners' three days on, three days off income was higher than four days pay and no dole.

Roy Mason was responsible for maintaining and repairing machinery and on one particular occasion he spent 27 hours working on a vital breakdown job underground. Eventually his family turned up at the pit-head to find out what had happened to him. Every few hours a bottle of water and sandwiches were sent down to him. His snap usually consisted of a bottle of water and four slices of bread and lard, worse than a

Left: Lord Mason.

prisoner's diet. Pork dripping was a luxury and, working in a confined space with a one-way air flow, the rest of the men soon realised what he was eating. The snap was wrapped in paper (many miners could not afford a snap tin) and on reaching the face he would tie a piece of string round the food and suspend it from a girder to try to hoodwink the mice. Mice were all over the workings, having hitched a lift in the sacks of grain sent down for the pit ponies in the underground stables.

At 23 he was elected a union branch committee man. He had been studying mechanical engineering on a day release course. On nationalisation in 1947 the NCB introduced a system of six days pay for a five day working week, provided miners worked for the five days. The proposal was introduced because of a shortage of coal and because of absenteeism. Because of the day release course, he missed a shift every week and the family could not afford

Below: Lord Mason, Minister of Power.

to lose the money. He asked the union to do something about it, nothing happened and he missed his examinations. So he contacted the MP for Hemsworth, Mr Horace Holmes, who persuaded the Government to amend the Act. To shake-up the union he stood for election and became a committee man. At 25 he was elected branch delegate. In 1953 he was elected MP for Barnsley, determined to improve society, an ambition he had nurtured since the death of his mother at an early age.

Ernest Bamford

Retired miner Mr Ernest Bamford is proud of the fact that he spent all his working life in the pit and said: "I have done more miles on my knees than most marathon runners have done on their feet."

Eighty-six years old Ernest Bamford, of Waddington Road, Pogmoor, started work in 1914 at Church Lane screens (Dodworth Colliery). When he moved to North Gawber Colliery he was to remain there for 35 years and was involved in the 1935 explosion in which nineteen men were killed. One of the men, Albert Ibberson, managed to write a message in chalk as he lay crippled. "I will never forget the words he wrote," said Ernest, "It was a message to his wife, 'Farewell Fanny, my love.'"

A Deputy, he was involved in the subsequent inquiry into the disaster. The inquiry concluded the pit had been seriously lacking in ventilation and it was agreed massive alterations to the system were necessary.

"Miners were the salt of the earth. They treated each other like brothers and were always willing to help each other. I knew all the men at the pit by name." For Ernest the annual concert at Sheffield City Hall stands as a fine example of the community spirit among miners. "It is fantastic to listen to the colliery bands and choirs."

Anonymous

An anonymous miner aged 81, who lives in Doncaster Road, remembers miners fainting from lack of air, and having to drink pints of water because of the heat down the pit. He started work in 1919 on the same day as his brother, who had just returned from the First World War. After working as a face worker for 47 years, he retired in 1970, receiving a lump sum of £203 when he left the pit. "Human beings were never made to go underground; they turned into animals when they went down a pit and became slaves."

Albert Haynes

The day sailors arrived at the 'watercress pit' (it earned its nickname because it was so wet) are recalled by Albert Haynes, aged 78, of High

Street, Grimethorpe. The pit (Grimethorpe's sister pit at Ferrymoor) was flooded and the navy were called in because there was a shortage of labour as a result of the First World War.

"I remember them arriving in their bell-bottom trousers and the word got round that the navy had arrived. The sailors went round the village handing out tins of bully beef to the children."

The watercress pit was one of the smallest in the coalfield. "The shaft was 90 yards deep and from the surface you could shout to someone in the pit bottom."

He recalls the strikes of 1921, 1926 and 1947 — which started at Grimethorpe — mainly because of the hot weather. "Miners were coal picking behind Deputy Row in 1921 and they were as brown as berries and the heat was so intense it melted the tarmac on the roads. In 1947, after nationalisation, management increased miners' work stint without telling them. More coal was produced but the men did not get any more pay, so they came out on strike and it became known as the stint strike."

Albert worked at Grimethorpe Colliery which produced coal known as Barnsley Bed Hards: "Our concessionary coal consisted of lumps as big as a television set."

Alf Parker

During 50 years spent working down the mines, Alf Parker tackled virtually every job that was going. Now 77 year old, Alf, of Gerald Crescent, Kendray, started work in 1924 at Wombwell Main and then worked at Mitchell Main, Wombwell, and Barnsley Main until it closed in 1967. He spent his last years at Barrow Colliery, retiring in 1974.

"I started off at Wombwell Main which was an easy pit. I soon found out what mining was all about when I moved to Barnsley Main in 1925. I did not like the time I spent at Mitchell Main and I lasted a couple of months there. The area I worked in was red hot and the ventilation was awful. It was like working in an oven."

He was a member of the rescue team and was called in when there was an explosion at Barnsley Main. Officials were examining the pit after a fire, but when the stoppings were removed there was an explosion. "One of my friends, Stan Parry, was a deputy at the time. I brought him out of the pit with a face like a tomato after he had been left for dead." In his 50 year career he did not escape injury and an incident with a pit pony left him with two broken ribs, although his broken nose was caused by a spade which he accidentally jumped on. "The most enjoyable time I spent down the pit were the last eight years. Until I retired I worked seven days a week driving the paddy at Barrow, and the manager ordered a specially made seat for me. It was the best job I ever had down the pit."

John Grayson

The 1926 miners' lock-out was a glorious time for young men without responsibilities. Like miners in the 1984/85 miners' strike, some of them experienced weeks of uninterrupted sunny weather for the first time in years. At Wombwell, where he lived, the public health inspector reported that the health of miners actually improved during the dispute. They may not have had enough to eat but the fresh air, the warmth and exercise did them a world of good.

"We came out of the pit in May and did not go back until November. It was the best time of my life," said the eighty-three years old. "My father had a job on the council and we did not feel the pinch like other families. We spent our time playing sport and walking." He remembers a miner with a motor-bike travelling on to the moors to steal sheep and miners waiting at a spot where the trains had to slow down so they could steal food and goods off the wagons.

His favourite miners' leader was Joe Hall, from Lundhill, Wombwell, whom he recalls being carried shoulder high through the streets of Wombwell to Brampton where he made a speech to a large gathering of miners. "A lot of miners worshipped Hall who was capable of making rousing speeches. The mounted Police were at Brampton and at one point it looked as if things would get nasty. A horse and cart carrying a load of bricks came down the street and I expected the miners grabbing the bricks and throwing them at the Police. But nothing happened. At other times the Police were brutes. The authorities must have chosen the biggest Policemen they could find to send to Barnsley. If three miners were walking down the street together, the Police would disperse them. The Police were used to escort 'black-legs' from the pits to their homes. I remember one black-leg who lived at Cortonwood. When he got to the safety of his home, he would turn and challenge the miners to a fight."

Arthur Akeroyd

Arthur Akeroyd started work on the screens at Barnsley Main Colliery in 1925 but within a few months the miners were locked out and he went coal picking at Pogmoor, charging 6d. a bag for 'spitting coal' (so called because it contained bits of pot and other objects which spat in the fire) and 1s. for riddled fuel; and at Silkstone Fall which worked during the dispute, and at what was known as the Bluebell Seam in Dodworth Road, where he was sometimes chased by Policemen.

"It was a glorious time — the weather was beautiful and I was sixteen," said Arthur, a retired pit winder who now lives in Shirland Avenue, Athersley. In a way he had been lucky for before the lock out he had worked on the surface, where most of the men were members of the General and Municipal Workers Union; his union paid strike money whereas the miners' union ran out of funds within four weeks.

"During the General Strike there was some trouble in the Gas Nook, Barnsley, where a bus was turned over. The TUC said all transport workers had to stop work but this bus was still operating." More than 50 years later he portrayed one of the miners' leaders in 1926, W G Richardson, in the BBC television series, "Days of Hope."

In 1928 most of the surface workers transferred to the Miners' Federation, although they did not receive the same perks as underground workers. "When the underground workers paid their contributions, the union officials gave them a Woodbine but the surface workers received nothing."

Thomas Franks

The tough muscular world of mining was in the blood of Thomas Franks (74), who spent 49 years in the industry. The former Woolley Colliery miner had the strength — and knack — to lift half ton tubs back on to the underground rails. And he was prepared to work seven days a week, often in terrible conditions and often in danger.

He saw three men killed in separate accidents and after finding one buried he nearly gave up the job. He was buried twice, broke a leg and had numerous injuries; but it never dampened his appetite for hard work and the pits. Working down the pit had its compensations. During one week in 1948 he earned £25, blue-chip earnings when £7 was regarded as a decent wage. But he had to work over the Easter holidays — with double shifts on Easter Tuesday — to hit the jackpot.

"The job has got easier over the years; during the period before my retirement I had to carry the tackle (belting, timber and girders) for men working on a heading and I was still working harder than the younger men."

His most embarrassing moment: he was called to the manager's office for alleged absenteeism, a serious offence during the Second World War, during which discipline was as tight as in the army. "It was all a mistake — I had worked six months without having a day off."

George Henry Taylor

George Henry Taylor (72), Sheffield Road, went down the pit at thirteen and a half working as a pony driver. When he was seventeen he was buried in the pit and went to Beckett Hospital, Barnsley, where he was encased in plaster. It took him two years to recover and as a

consequence his wedding had to be postponed. He spent 50 years in the industry, 25 of which were at Monk Bretton. He also worked at Barnsley Main, missing the explosions of 1942 and 1947 through illness.

Walter Darlington

Walter Darlington (77), Doncaster Road, believes he had a lucky escape. He went down the pit at sixteen, in 1926, for which he was paid £2 7s. a week. It came as a shock when after only seven weeks the miners were locked out in the 1926 dispute. Walter considers he was lucky as he quickly found work in a butcher's shop and never returned to the pit.

John Haughton

John Haughton (70), Pontefract Road, was working at Rockingham Colliery, Hoyland Common, when the roof caved in and killed two of his pals. John had been working with one of them the previous day and when the news went round Barnsley Main Colliery his brother thought John had been killed.

"The two men had been doing some repair work when four girders dropped: 40 tons of metal and earth fell on them. We spent most of the day digging them out. I was off work a week because I was so upset."

John Haughton worked in the Lower Fenton Seam. Some of the seams were so close that debris fell from one to another. "In 1948 I remember finding a racing pink newspaper, dated 1912, which had come from the Top Fenton seam which had been worked in the early years of the century and which had not been worked for years. The odd coal tub came down too. From Rockingham you could make your way into Barrow, Skiers Spring, Platts Common and Pilley Collieries. We kept the airway clear in the old Pilley Colliery and to do this work we had to use the disused shaft. So much water came down the Pilley shaft we were glad to reach the surface." He worked for 42 years in the mines, at Rockingham, Barnsley Main and Barrow. "There was nothing but hard work down a pit — my health has never been better since I left."

Edward Slater

Edward Slater remembers his father's body being carried from a horse-drawn ambulance into his house in 1921, after an accident at Barnsley Main Colliery. Consequently seven year old Edward did not look forward to a life in a mine.

When Edward left school there were no jobs outside mining and even the pits were on short time. So Edward and his brothers, John and Thomas, went to work at Barnsley Main, where their father was killed. In Edward's case history nearly repeated itself. On 7 May, 1947, he was working on a new face when there was an explosion, killing nine men and injuring twenty-three. At his home in Samuel Road, Gawber, he said: "I remember cap lamps were coming in and I was fortunate enough to get one. The force of the blast took the helmet straight off my head. I had my back to the blast so I was thrown flat on my face. I pulled my cable to retrieve my helmet and light but it made no difference, everything was a mass of dust. My mate and I scrambled along the tailgate by instinct and we were on our way to the pit bottom when we suddenly went cold: our skin had shrivelled as a result of the flash."

Edward was in the ambulance room when the first of the stretchers arrived. "That was enough for me. I left and went to see my own doctor. I think I was the only man in the explosion not to go to hospital. Barnsley Main claimed my father and nearly claimed me."

Eli Sumnall

Mrs Winifred Gillespie (80) of Scarborough, said time could not dim the memories of the old Yorkshire Mineworkers' Association. Her father, the late Eli Sumnall, was secretary of the Wharncliffe Woodmoor 1/2/3 branch of the YMA for more than thirty years. The union and the miners were his life. Always the knock-knock on the door: "Is your dad in?" or "Can you help, Eli?"

"Ill and breathless with pneumoconiosis, maimed, disabled, human beings, denied recognition of liability for their injuries. My father spent demoralising hours arguing for their rights. Many frail old miners kept in the union so as to qualify for the death benefit of £6 to help bury them. So important was the union to him that in 1933 he took us to Tolpuddle in Dorset for the commemoration of the 100th anniversary of the Tolpuddle martyrs, the men who formed the first trade union. What depth of feeling to stand where they once stood. Our names are in the Book of Remembrance.

The nationalisation of the mines in 1947 was his dream, and when the flag was raised at the pithead he quoted one of the Proverbs from the Bible to the effect that 'hope deferred made the heart sick, but when the desire came it turned out to be the Tree of Life'. And so it seemed for a while but disillusionment set in and in the end he said that they had changed the name but the bosses were the same.

"Today (1987) there is no trace of Wharncliffe Woodmoor but thank God we still have the union."

Albert Clarkson

Albert Clarkson has bitter memories of one strike which took place at Cortonwood Colliery during the Second World War. Late in 1941 the Cortonwood Colliery Company successfuly applied for Government permission to cut the face workers' wages by one-third. The company claimed the reduction was necessaery because one of the seams had ceased to be viable. Miners downed tools in protest and held out for five hard weeks over Christmas and the New Year before going back on slightly better terms. They had recouped 2d. of the 6d. cut. Albert Clarkson, aged 73, of Fearnhouse Crescent, Hoyland Common, a face worker at the colliery said: "We had been paid 1s. 6 1/2d. a ton for the coal we produced, but the company suddenly turned round and said they could not pay it. They had previously introduced a new system of cutting coal in the Silkstone seam which made it look as if we were unproductive, but the new system was not working properly."

To support his wife and two children Albert used to retrieve old wreaths from a refuse tip in Hoyland, after which he would strip them down, re-decorate them with holly from the wood and then sell them to mourners.

"In those days we had what we called Parish Relief. The first time I applied for it was four weeks after the strike had started and I received twenty two shillings. The man who was handing it out said that if I spent it on anything but food I would be sent to prison. After the strike we were taken to Rotherham Magistrates Court by the company for going on strike. We were fined by the magistrates and one of them said if he had enough power he would line us up against a wall and shoot us for being unpatriotic. But that wasn't true — we were as patriotic as everyone else."

Ernest Woodhead

Ernest Woodhead (21), was a hard and willing worker but, for some reason, he was unwilling to travel from his home in St John's Terrace, Buckley Street, to the colliery on 4 February, 1943. His reluctance was not shared by his mother, Harriet, for words were exchanged and he set off to work. That was the last time Mrs Woodhead saw him alive. Shortly after 3.45 pm that day Ernest was working with William Henry Glover, aged 47, of Churchfield Lane, Kexborough, trying to erect a roof support girder at Woolley Colliery after the firing of six shots when three tons of stone fell on him.

Ernest suffered a fractured skull and died almost immediately. One of the first to be informed was his father, Frank, who was working in a different part of the pit the same day. The man with Ernest, William Glover, a ripper, died of asphyxia. At the inquest there was a difference of opinion between H M Inspector, a Mr Green, and the deputy in charge that day, Mr Charles Hinchcliffe Jackson, of Bridge Street, Darton. Green believed the additional timber safety props should have been placed in position before the shots were fired but Jackson believed every reasonable safeguard had been taken and the quickest and

safest way had been to set the girder as soon as possible after the firing of the shots. The verdict at the inquest: death by misadventure. Some weeks later colliery proprietors Fountain and Burnley paid the family £150 under the Workmen's Compensation Act. That sum was the equivalent of Ernest's wages for 25 weeks.

Alfred Smith

Sixty-seven-year-old Alfred Smith, of Darton, worked at Woolley Colliery for twenty-six years, beginning in 1933 at the age of fourteen; in 1936 he began work underground. On his first day he had to walk and crawl three and a half miles to get to the coal face. "At the end of my first shift I did not realise everyone had gone and the deputy had to come looking for me. He said he had been looking for me for half an hour."

He still has nightmares over his brushes with death. "On one occasion there were two of us in the cage when the engine man must have been given the wrong signal, believing he was dropping coal. The cage dropped almost one thousand feet at such a speed we hardly had time to be frightened but the bad air meant we could not breathe properly. The shock hit us when we reached the bottom and we had to be hauled out of the cage."

On another occasion when the lockers failed to hold the tubs, and he had not altered the points, he was nearly responsible for the death of twenty men. "The tubs were heading for a cage holding twenty men and I could not stop them. My cries of 'runaway!' warned them and they managed to get out of the cage before the tubs hit it. That could have been an awful accident and it would have been my fault."

The best part of the day when he was a lad was the ride back to the stables. "At the end of the shift, against all the rules, I used to ride back to the stable on my pony and I only banged by head and fell off once. I do remember on one occasion knocking the Under Manager over when I was riding back to the stables and I had a lot of explaining to do. The pit manager fined me five bob." Alf Smith left Woolley in 1959 with a lung ailment.

Ralph Dyson

Ralph Dyson (59), Highstone Road, Worsbrough Common, recalls the humour and comradeship as well as the hard work underground. In 1942 he left school on a Friday and started work at Old Carlton Colliery on the Monday. Later he worked at the other Wharncliffe Woodmoor Colliery, Barnsley Main, Wombwell Main, Grimethorpe, Haigh, Barrow, Woolley and North Gawber as well as two private pits, Brook's at Silkstone and Robinson's at Cawthorne.

When I started conditions were primitive, but they improved after nationalisation. The trouble was they nationalised the pits but they did not nationalise the bosses, and the number of bosses increased after 1947."

Every pit had its hate list of deputies. One deputy, known as 'Black Charlie' at Barnsley Main, was injured in an accident and none of the men helped him: "He was rotten — rotten to everyone."

There were plenty of characters. During the war it was not easy to get transferred to another pit. The manager at Haigh Colliery was a rough diamond who had worked his way up from the coal face. He had no finesse and he was well schooled in the art of ungentle persuasion. Ralph Dyson wanted to leave the pit because of the conditions but the manager outwitted him. One day he went to the manager's office determined to get his transfer. Convinced that he had won, he went to the offices with a note from the manager, expecting to be paid up, only to discover that the note was for a new set of picks. On another occasion the manager made him feel guilty by telling him: "Things can't be that bad here — you have put some weight on and you have colour in your cheeks." Eventually he did leave.

Managers did not get their own way all the time. At another pit the area manager was on his rounds when he spotted two lads asleep. Poking one with his stick, he asked: "Do you know who I am?" Rubbing his eyes, the lad turned to his mate and said: "There's a bloke here who doesn't know who he is."

In the old days tragedy was just round the corner. Ralph Dyson's father rarely had a shift off work but one day he met his relatives and they all ended up at the club at Long Row, Carlton. His father missed the shift; his mates who had been drinking with him went underground and they were killed.

Ralph's career came to an end when a large stone and metal bar pinned him to the ground in a kneeling position at North Gawber, the deputy rescuing him by removing the dirt from underneath his knees. In the ambulance room the medical staff asked him to go to hospital but he refused because he was needed at home and struggled to the bus. His back was badly injured and later he had to be treated in hospital and was off work for three years.

John Allen

John Allen said he would do someone a favour — and as a result almost died. While working at Wentworth Silkstone Colliery, near Stainborough, in November 1960, a machine amputated his left leg and almost severed the right. John of Devonshire Drive, was working with his son-in-law on development work when the accident occurred. "It was the end of the shift — ten minutes past one and we decided to go for the paddy train. The afternoon shift was following on and I changed my mind, deciding to do them a favour. I thought I would push the machine back to give them a good start. We put a rope round the machine, tightened it and got out of the way. The machine was switched on, but the rope broke and the seven foot jib swung round and caught me with its sharp teeth. My left leg was taken off at the knee and my right leg was almost cut off."

He managed to struggle over the tension (a belt drum) and crawled 30 yards down the face. By then the rescue team was on its way. They gave him a seven pint blood transfusion. "I was conscious and I could not feel any pain. As the minutes went by I decided I had a chance if I saw daylight."

In the ambulance room on the surface he still couldn't feel any pain and men were going down like ninepins because they could not stand the sight of his mangled body. In the hospital casualty department he finally lost consciousness — for a week — and was in hospital for six weeks.

After learning to walk again with the aid of artificial limbs he had a number of jobs in mining, retiring in 1975 from Dodworth Colliery. "It has been a long hard slog - if I didn't have my wife I would have gone under."

It was not the first tragedy in his life, for his brother was killed by a runaway tub in 1939, the family receiving a lump sum of £90 in compensation.

"I was a seven days a week man at the pit and I have gone in to work on a Sunday evening but if I had my life over again, I wouldn't work like that again."

Derek 'Chocker' Reeves

The "powder monkey" strike at Darfield Main Colliery started Derek 'Chocker' Reeves on his union career. As a teenager 'Chocker' and the other pit lads wanted one shilling and five pence a can to carry the explosive powder down the pit, a job colliers would not do. The tin carrier was known as 'a powder monkey' and the lads downed tools when managers declined to concede the payment. At the end of the week-long strike a compromise was reached — the men had to carry the cans.

At sixteen (1955) he sought election as a union man and lost by seven votes. He was a likeable militant and the lads caused so much trouble

that the manager, with a twinkle in his eye, put them on the 2pm to 10 pm shift. The pubs in those days closed at 10.30 pm and the manager thought by restricting their drinking time he would turn them into moderates.

Life down the pit was never dull and the lads indulged in jolly japes. Chocker once attached a bucket of water to a hook, above head height. Then he attached a rope to the bucket and hid in an alcove underground. His mates got a whiff of his plan to shower them with water and did not come near; instead an unsuspecting miner turned up. Unable to see the miner in the dark, but hearing his footsteps, Chocker went into action and the miner ended up soaked to the skin with an upturned bucket on his head.

Dashing out of the alcove with a raucous 'I've got you!' Chocker found himself face to face with what appeared to be an Australian bush ranger, complete with metal helmet. A muffled voice inside the bucket sighed: 'The lad must be mad.'

On another occasion the pit knock-out cricket team accepted an invitation to play a game at an RAF training college. The upper-class RAF officers thought they had invited the Yorkshire Council side from Mitchell and Darfield. The pit team arrived in an old van enveloped in clouds of choking exhaust fumes and as the motley crew jumped out of the van with their Albert Hirst shopping bags full of gear, one of the officers was heard to say: "I say, is that a cricket team?"

The pit team included a sixty-year-old miner who tried to put his pads on back to front, and a couple of jokers who sat down on the boundary smoking, when they were supposed to be fielding. They were out classed to say the least and after the match the teams were enjoying refreshments when one of the jokers, Alan Beck, strutted up and down with a cricket box clasped to his mouth declaring: "Angels one five, bandits at four o'clock."

Chocker was so embarrassed he breathed a sigh of relief when they were on their way home — although he believes the match is still talked about down among the gin and tonics in the RAF mess.

*Derek 'Chocker' Reeves was elected Barnsley area agent of the NUM in the early 1980s, being responsible for more than ten pits and 15,000 men. He retired in 1991 and died in 1993, aged 54. He was a born comedian and much loved by miners. At the funeral service Wombwell Parish Church was filled to capacity and the mourners included Arthur Scargill, President of the NUM.

"The Holocaust and Martyrdom of the Mine."

DEDICATED TO HUMANITY BY
EDWARD A. RYMER, Monk Bretton, near Barnsley, 1903.

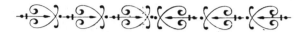

Deep beneath the solid earth,
Where volcanoes have their birth,
There engraved on leaves of stone,
Pictured ages past and gone.

Where natures vast and boundless store
Enrich the earth from shore to shore,
And countless ages leave behind,
A sublime record for mankind.

The nations speak with lightning power,
Engines eternal space devour;
And art has wrought a mighty scroll,
From energy stored up in coal.

In searching out this boundless worth,
From east to west, from south to north,
The mining toiler wins the coal,
And commerce sends from pole to pole.

Bold science with a stern command
In triumph conquors every land,
Her mandates rush across the line,
With blood and treasure from the mine.

From British Isle to Austral plains,
Britain still her power maintains,
From India to Canadian shores,
The miner o'er the world explores.

At his grim toil, faced with death,
Inhaling poison with each breath,
While every impulse of his soul,
Reminds him of the funeral pall.

The fiery demon lurks around,
In sunless regions underground,
And subtle gases fill the air,
Menacing destruction everywhere.

Lo! the pit has fired and flames arise,
The mine fiend mocks its victims cries,
While thundering echoes shake the ground,
And shrieks are heard for miles around.

The aged father groans with fear,
The loving mother tears her hair,
And children fly amidst the gloom,
To yonder pit—their father's tomb.

The stricken widow faints with grief,
Convulsed amidst a scene of death;
And children clutch her struggling form,
And wail at every parting groan.

Behold! the volunteers descend:
As pilots in the gulf of death;
With love and hope their spirits blend,
While choke damp poisons every breath.

With fire and smoke and dead around,
Those heroes of the burning mine
A ransom give till all is found,
And makes a record so sublime.

There's none to help them in their need,
None to cheer them in their deed,
Doves of hope to those beneath,
And pilots in the gulf of death.

'Tis natures last and only stay,
Oh aid them angels on their way,
And bless them for their noble deed,
To help the miner in his need.

If danger be by fire or flood,
The sons of Britain know the word;
Help and rescue, brings warriors forth,
To bless the land that gave them birth.

Let justice plead and mercy crave
For England's noble sons, and brave,
Whose deeds enshrined on scroll of fame
Makes hallowed grand Old England's name.

Oh England! shall thy sons so brave,
Sink helpless to a pauper's grave?
For statesmen shudder at the scene
Lamented by the nation's Queen!

Go see within yon gloomy cot
The crowning risk of the miner's lot,
And measure the sorrow of that devoted wife
Then grasp the struggle of the miner's life.

Arrest, oh Britain this saddening tale,
Nor waft it o'er the morning gale,
That hapless victims find a tomb,
In struggling with the miners' doom.

Scrapbook

Below: Houghton Main Colliery, 1890s.
Loaned by Mr W. Milford, Cudworth.

Right: A pit in the Milton area of Hoyland.
G. Beedan.

Below: Mitchell Main, Wombwell.

Above: Typical miners' cottages.
J. Goodchild Collection

Left: Darfield girls inspect a load of coal, 1920s.
R.J. Short.

Below: Haircut in a back yard, Low Valley, 1920s or 1930s.
R.J. Short.

Above: Houghton Main, 1940s.
R.J. Short.

Right: Roy Mason, MP, inspects a coal face.
British Coal.

Above: Houghton Main.
R.J. Short.

Left: Billingley Drift Mine.
Mr M. Hopkinson, Darfield.

Index